WILD THINGS

REG PRESLEY

WILD THINGS

THEY DON'T TELL US

metro

Published by Metro Publishing Ltd, 3 Bramber Court,
2 Bramber Road, London W14 9PB, England

First published in the UK in hardback in 2002

ISBN 1 84358 043 8

British Library Cataloguing-in-Publication Data: A catalogue record for this book is
available from the British Library.

Design by ENVY

Printed and bound in Great Britain by CPD (Wales)

1 3 5 7 9 10 8 6 4 2

Papers used by Metro Publishing Ltd are natural, recyclable products made from
wood grown in sustainable forests. The manufacturing processes conform to the
environmental regulations of the country of origin.

Pictures reproduced by kind permission of Colin Andrews, Aulis Publishers/NASA,
Cambridge Evening News, Four Corners Vision, *San Diego Union Tribune* and
Busty Taylor. Every attempt has been made to contact the relevant copyright-holders,
but some were unobtainable. We would be grateful if the appropriate
people could contact us.

CONTENTS

ACKNOWLEDGEMENTS

This book was not conceived to make money. It was conceived to inform, to place the people who read it in a position to find the truth out for themselves. Only the individual can find the truth that suits their reasoning. I have been helped by people willing to share their thoughts and findings with anyone willing to listen. Each one of them has followed specific avenues of investigation. My idea in writing this book was to seek out and bring together all the avenues of their work and try to form the ultimate picture of their findings, so that people that do not have time can see where it could all be leading. If this book only enlightens one person, then we are all, possibly, a step nearer to the truth.

Gargantuan thanks to:
Colin Andrews, who first took me down the path of reasoning

7

about the crop circle phenomenon and to the friendship we have formed throughout the years and also for his input into the book. Also to ever ready Busty Taylor, willing at the drop of a hat to help anyone, for his input in the book. To farmers Tim and Polly Carson, for letting the hordes of crop circle enthusiasts on to their land without so much as a murmur of discontent, and also to any like-minded farmers in the region. To best-selling author Laurence Gardner for a goldmine of information from his *Bloodline Of The Holy Grail* and *Genesis Of The Grail Kings* – in the future I hope to work with him on a TV series on his subjects. To David Hudson, for courage and perseverance on his long trek to seek out the truth about gold powder and a possible cure for all ills. To Graham Hancock – who's ahead of the swim! To the late Royal Raymond Rife for the same effect, but through a different avenue of research. To Richard Hoagland for bringing attention to the Monument on Mars. To Errol Torun for how the planets may work. To the amazing work of amateur Egyptologist John West, who discovered that the Sphinx is at least 15,000 years old. To Dr Richard Thomson and Michael Cremo for their co-authored book on forbidden archaeology. To Virginia Steen-McIntyre, PhD; J D Whitney, geologist; Carl Baugh, anthropologist; Dr Dale Peterson, MD; Don Patton, geologist; plus miners from South Africa for letting the world know that mankind could date from at least as far back as 2.8 billion years ago. To Derrel Sims and Dr Roger Leir for their work on getting proof of abductions and alien implants. To Stanton Freidman for all his devotion and persistence on the Roswell crash and on the whole UFO subject. To Ray Santilli for awakening everyone to the fact that there is still something out there, and for being a pain in everyone's butt. To the cameraman from Florida who says he took the alien autopsy footage at Roswell – please come forward, you'll be a hero. To the late great Colonel Corso who was at the Pentagon in 1947 and worked on artefacts from the Roswell crashed UFO. To Steven Greer for relentless persistence to make the American government come clean about what they know or don't know, through his Disclosure Project. To Bob Dean for coming forward about his UFO knowledge of SHAPE. To Marina Popovitch, a truly warm and loveable person, and Russian cosmonaut. To Professor Valerie Uveroff – keep up the good work. To Alex the Russian lorry driver. To Jim Hurtak, in tune with the world. To film director Marcus Thompson for having the faith to make *A Place to Stay* a love story with crop circle connections, and allowing me the privilege of playing a small role. To Marcus Allen who runs the UK *NEXUS* magazine for keeping me informed about the A to Z of the weird. To David Percy, many thanks. To David Parker, thanks for the photograph. To amateur astronomer Chris Trubridge for his discovery of the star system above and its connection with Avebury. To Germany's Michael Hesseman – born to get to the bottom of everything and tell the world. And to Adam for having faith. For stories and sightings to producer Richard Niles, Ray Dorset of Mungo Jerry, Clem Curtis of The Foundations, Pete Lucas of The Troggs, Noddy Holder of Slade, and last but not least Sting. To Joyce Bowls and the late Ted Pratt for sharing their story. To Brian Tubb for his phenomenal observation of geese. To Gary Keel and family. To James and Yvonne Withers for good memories. To Tom and Kerry Blower for staging conferences. To Irene Bott for the same. To Adrian and June and all at the Barge Inn in Honey Street, Wiltshire, for their services to the cause. To Patrick at the Red Lion at Avebury for the same. To Matt Williams who finds it hard to keep out of trouble, but can always mend a sick computer. To the only Yank who can find and pinpoint anybody's camcorder, on a tripod, within a ten-mile radius, in the pitch dark, while they are actually filming a UFO, kick it and place obscene language on the soundtrack all within a few seconds – the one and only Peter Sorensen. The Americans should have used him as a pilot in Afghanistan with that kind of accuracy, but he's always welcome back. To the hoaxers who keep us amused while we are searching for the real ones. To my daughter Karen who took my place on night watches when I was performing. To my son Jason who didn't give up on my grammar! To Phamie MacDonald, a work force to be reckoned with in her own right who fought alongside me to get the book out on time, a great graphic designer. To international artist David Penfound for the artwork on the book cover, above and beyond the call of duty. See his work at davidpenfound.com. To my wife Brenda who as yet doesn't believe in UFOs even though she has seen one! And last but not least to John Blake of Blake Publishing for having the insight to know that you, the public, have the right to know all possibilities.

I thank you all and wish you good hunting – for the truth, that is!

FOREWORD

There was a time when most people probably thought that Leonardo da Vinci should have been fitted up for a straitjacket because he suggested that one day we might fly in helicopters and travel underwater in submarines. There was a time when popular opinion would have locked Christopher Columbus away for daring to suggest that you could sail right around the world instead of off the edge. There's always a time when visionaries are in danger of being stowed away in padded cells, or at best laughed at, and I guess Reg Presley is no different.

Whether his beliefs and predictions turn out to be science fiction speculation or prophesy leading us to a brave new world, one filled with benign beings from other planets who have come to help us, and guide our day to day lives – who knows? Whilst, there are some who will never be convinced beyond all reasonable doubt that what is in this book is anything more than speculation, I've yet to hear anyone, scientist, politician or cleric, who could convince me that there definitely aren't alien beings 'out there' somewhere. If I were to put money on it, I'm sure that the laws of probability would weigh in on Reg's side, against the majority who insist on doing a Greta Garbo and wanting to be alone.

Of course there's no way that anyone at the moment can either prove or disprove that there's anything else out there. But me? I'd rather live in a world where there's the slightest chance that Reg Presley's dreams are reality, that live in determined isolation on this little rock of ours. I don't pretend to know if Reg is right or wrong, all I do know is that I want him to be right. One thing is for sure though, and that is that if we ever want world peace, we'd better hope that he is, because it seems to me as though we're in desperate need of some outside help.

Prophet or madman? – Read it and decide for yourself.

Adam Faith
2002

INTRODUCTION

As individuals we each have the ability to perceive the world slightly differently from others. Information that we collect in our minds slowly builds those perceptions into whatever suits our way of interpreting the world. We are helped and hindered in our process of learning by academics, who interpret their findings slightly differently from how we ourselves may.

For instance, if we find graffiti on a wall, we would not dream that the person who put it there actually built the wall. Yet when Egyptologists find Egyptian hieroglyphs on the walls of pyramids, they automatically assume the Egyptians built them. The Sphinx, according to Egyptologists, was built around the same time as the pyramids. Yet John West, a self taught Egyptologist, recently discovered that the weathering on the Sphinx is water weathering. The kind of rain needed for this type of weathering to occur has not fallen in the region for about 11,000 years.

When an old campfire is found near ancient monuments such as Stonehenge or Avebury, and the fire is dated to 4,000 years ago, do you conclude that the people who lit the fire placed the stones there? Archaeologists do. In many cases, carbon dating is used to date objects found near these sites. Carbon dating is gradually being proved unreliable. This in turn will change evidence, and hence change our perceptions.

I have noticed throughout my life that scientists change some of their ideas about every ten years. So what we are being told today may not be true in ten years' time. When I was at school we were taught that the Earth came from the Sun. Twenty years ago the Big Bang theory was accepted. Now scientists believe in a collection of gases. When will they ever be right? The answer has to be never. All that scientists, and especially physicists, can have are opinions based on knowledge at that moment in time, and I include myself in this.

As yet, the study of crop formations and UFOlogy is not a science. Therefore, although some scientists may be looking into these phenomena, they cannot be seen to be doing so by their fraternity. Behind the scenes, work is being carried out and some questions are being answered. We may still have a long way to go. Who knows?

However, I do not believe anyone can spend 12 years, as I have, studying crop formations and the UFO phenomenon, without forming strong opinions on the whole subject, although the trial – as it were – is still ongoing, and the evidence still coming in. One conclusion I have come to is that if you wish to know all that is going on around you on this planet, you are the only one that can get to the truth. You as an individual have much work to do. You have many books to read, many lectures to visit, and should have a truly open mind to begin with. You will have to listen to much misinformation, but be able to siphon off small pieces of good information that will, from time to time, be hidden there within it. There will be people paid by governments and private individuals that will come forward as though to help, but with other motives. There will also be the glory seekers, in it for 15 minutes of fame. Government bodies will try to keep us from the truth. Our only chance of winning that truth is for the believers to become the majority.

CHAPTER 1

Had someone told me 12 years ago, that I would be writing a book about crop circles, UFOs or anything verging on the paranormal, I would have told them they had more chance of Tony Blair voting Conservative at the next election. However, after 12 years of intensive research into these and other phenomena, I have no alternative but to believe that humanity is on the brink of one of the greatest discoveries of all time. That is a very profound statement to make, and I would not make it if I did not feel I had the evidence to back it up.

It appears, at least since the war, that consecutive world governments have spent millions of pounds on investigations into the UFO phenomenon and have documented evidence of their existence. The lengths to which these governments will go to hide this information never cease to amaze me. Until now it has been relatively easy for them to do this, because they have owned 99 per cent of all the surveillance equipment. However, this has changed over recent years and sophisticated technology is now in the public domain, in the shape of camcorders, digital cameras, mobile phone scanners, GPS and so on. For a nominal fee, you can now zoom in to anywhere on the planet via satellite. So gone are the days of only blurred photographs of UFOs, it will not be long before someone, somewhere, films the landing of an extra-terrestrial spacecraft, and possibly its occupants.

'Seeing is believing' had always been my motto. For this reason, in my youth I had big problems getting to grips with God. I could not see this all-powerful person (as we were led to believe) being able to keep his eye on everything we did. So rather than be out of step with the rest of mankind by not believing in God, I searched my mind for a logical answer. I now believe that God would be far better known and understood as chaos. Everything we humans know is born from chaos. Science says that in the beginning there was a big bang – that being the ultimate chaos. Trillions of particles being thrown out into the void of space, in every direction? *That's* chaos. Each of those particles being different in some way, each cooling to different temperatures? *That's* chaos. Only some of these rock particles being able to harbour life? That brings us to the biggest chaos of all – life itself. The chances of anything ever being born out of all of this are zillions to one. Even the vaginal passage of a woman has a disinfectant fluid which is secreted to prevent sperm, or any other foreign bodies, taking hold.

How could God let 32 schoolchildren plunge into a ravine in a school bus? What sins could they possibly be guilty of at five and six years old? And please don't give me that old 'God works in mysterious ways' routine. So with all this chaos in mind, I believe chance plays a major role in the game of life. And where better to play that game than hurtling through a void at thousands of miles an hour on a ball of rock that can fry or freeze you, dancing on tectonic plates that can destroy the ground beneath you, rained on by meteors and asteroids, right next door to a ball of fire that's slowly dying. A god that put us here would have to be one sick lizard. Surely no one in their right mind would put the children they loved in such danger as that which the human race is in.

It's at this point in my thinking that I begin to look for a more suitable word in the place of chaos, a softer word with some meaning. I suppose this is when most people would say God. I would say Nature or, even more comforting, Mother Earth. The Native American Indians have it right – they love Mother Earth, she holds all they need, even though they know how temperamental she can be. If I use the word God today, to me it means the essence of all the energy in the cosmos – not a thinking force, just one that occurs at random, as a result of whatever energy is at hand. The human race is part of this energy. We can affect the Earth, the Earth can affect us. Energy is never destroyed, it is only changed. So, when we humans finally succumb to whatever fate chaos throws at us, we shall become the energy for the next chaotic event.

It was not in my wildest imagination that by walking into a crop formation all my beliefs would be changed (see picture section). It was never the formations themselves that changed my beliefs. It was the work that went into research trying to discover what or who were the circle makers. The information I am about to share with you sent me on a learning curve that eventually changed my life.

CHAPTER 2

I t all began for me back in early August 1990. Although I was
aware of the existence of crop circles, I had not given the
matter much thought. It was not until a Sunday newspaper
covered a story on a huge crop formation in a wheatfield at
Alton Barnes, Marlborough, in Wiltshire, that I first decided to
take a look. In fact, as I read the report, I had a compelling
feeling that I should go.

It had been a long hot dry summer, and the weekend in
question was no exception. I entered the Pewsey Vale from the
south-east, and used the road that runs along the southern side
of east field where the crop formation was reported to be. In
case I missed it, I scoured the wheatfields to my right, which
run the length of the Pewsey Vale, and peter out beneath the
rolling chalk hills that meander their way through the
countryside to Devizes and beyond. As I reached the brow of a

small incline in the road, I looked across the valley and there, as though a giant pastry cutter had been at work, I saw my first crop formation.

I realised that I would get a much better view from the north side of east field, so I turned right at the next intersection, past the white horse, and headed on up towards the top of Knap Hill. At the top there is a small car park, which gives you a scenic view of the whole of the Pewsey Vale. I locked the car and ambled off down the hill in the warm August sunshine. There was a small caravan parked at the end of the track that led to the entrance of the field. Here the farmer was charging one pound to enter. This enabled us later, with information from the farmer, to establish that over 7,000 people had paid one pound each to investigate the crop formation for themselves.

People were beginning to gather by the small caravan, laughing and joking, and there was a sense of high spirits. They were swapping ideas and information, and there was a sense of camaraderie among them. I remember turning to the farmer and saying, 'Can you make the crop formation closer to the edge of the field next year, so we don't have so far to walk?' As I turned and looked down towards the crop formation, which ran 60 metres down the field, I felt the laugh was on me.

The first person I met and spoke to was Busty Taylor (see picture section). He had a camera around his neck, and in the briefcase that was open at his feet I noticed, among other things, a tape measure and a compass. He turned to me and said, 'So what do you think then?' I looked at him, smiled, and said, 'I was just going to ask you the same question.' That started a conversation lasting approximately two hours. During our conversation we became aware of a gentleman stood behind us, who was probably eavesdropping on what we were saying. He was wearing a rather old-fashioned crash helmet, and although I had not noticed one on my way down the hill, I imagined him to have an old moped parked somewhere on the road. I also noticed two wires hanging from his jacket pocket, which I recognised as being what some people use for dowsing. I had an immediate memory flash (see picture section).

As a young man I served an apprenticeship as a bricklayer, and at 17 I worked with an old bricklayer who was about to retire. We were driven to a field in the country where two houses were going to be built. Our first job when we reached the site was to find water. Our boss told us that a water pipe crossed the land, but we didn't know where. We searched for about ten minutes in the long grass near the road, looking for the usual water board sign, but found nothing.

Then suddenly, the old bricklayer took a penknife from his pocket and walked over to a hazel thicket. He peered up into the thin branches, then cut a Y-shaped piece of wood from the tree. He then walked back to the site, trimming off the unwanted leaves. He placed one of the two forks of wood in each hand and bent them around, so they looked like the handlebars of a bicycle that had been removed from their frame. He then began to walk diagonally across the land. Because of the length of the grass and the density at its base, he naturally lifted his legs higher than he would have done had he been walking on flatter terrain. It looked for all the world as though he was riding an invisible bicycle.

I confess, at that time I knew nothing about dowsing so I thought the old fellow had lost his marbles. Then suddenly he stopped, as the twig began to rise. I was told to mark the spot with a wooden stake, which I did. Then he did the same thing, but from another direction. As I hammered the next wooden stake into the ground, he told me that we would find the water pipe in a straight line beneath the two pegs, about 3 feet down. I hesitated for a moment, thought about it, then said, 'I'll dig the first hole, you dig the rest.' I can assure you, there were more than murmurs of discontent as I dug down into the ground.

When I got down to about 3 feet, metal hit metal and the shudder ricocheted up my arm as the spade hit the metal pipe. I could not believe what had happened. I fired question after question at him, trying to find out how he did it, and how it worked. I searched around in the long grass, looking for the discarded piece of wood that he had used. I found it, picked it up and bent it around in my hands as he had done, then I too walked across the ground, and was amazed that it worked for me. Then I started to experiment with the piece of wood. I held it tightly in my hands, but it still moved upwards. Then I gripped it even tighter, trying to keep it still, but the bark twisted off the wood with the force as it tried to rise. I could not believe the energy that was present. The old bricklayer showed me what to look for in the hazel thicket so that I could cut my own, and I have found water on several occasions since.

A limited amount of study has been carried out on dowsing over the years, but no one has yet come up with a satisfactory answer as to how and why it works.

I had never used metal dowsing rods, only wood, and never

for anything other than dowsing for water. So it was with a little apprehension that I asked the man in the crash helmet if I could use his rods to dowse the circle. I moved to the edge of the circle, placed a divining rod in each hand, and immediately the rods opened out in opposing directions. I then proceeded to walk across the circle. When I reached half way along the radius the rods swung back in, and crossed. When I reached the centre of the circle the rods swung back out again. The same thing happened on the way to the other side of the circle. I turned around and was about to make the same journey back across the circle when I noticed that a gusting breeze had developed. I thought that this could interfere with the action of the dowsing rods. As I proceeded to cross the circle, against this breeze, the rods crossed again, and I assumed there must be energy of some kind within the crop formation. With the rods still in my hands I walked between the two circles that were connected by a pathway of flattened wheat. The same thing happened again between the two circles, just as though there was an invisible circle between the two. Although none of us there knew what the dowsing rods were trying to tell us, we were all in agreement that a high energy was present in that crop formation – two weeks after it was laid down.

I handed the dowsing rods back to the gentlemen in the crash helmet. In turn he handed me a pamphlet from Circle Phenomena Research (CPR), and told me if I was interested to know more about the crop formations, these were the people to contact. I thanked him and Busty Taylor for their time, and left. I drove home very slowly that day, but my mind was acting as if it had been wired to a computer. I was frantically trying to get logical explanations for the questions I kept asking myself.

According to Busty, some people had seen simple circles as far back as 1976 (see picture section), but he personally had seen his first circle in 1985. Busty is a pilot, so why didn't he see his first crop circle until then? I suddenly had a thought. If crop circles and formations had been occurring during the course of the war, then aircraft returning to their bases flying low over the southern fields of England should have seen them. At that time they might have thought of them as coded messages laid down by spies for enemy aircraft. Although they may have kept that as a closely guarded secret during the war, I'm sure we would have known about it afterwards. Although several Second World War pilots were asked if they had seen any, the answer was always negative.

I also chewed over the idea of possible lightning strikes on the other side of the planet. By the time the energy had travelled 8,000 miles or so through the Earth and come out the other side, maybe it would still have enough power to lay the corn down in these strange patterns. If, indeed, that was how lightning worked. It's a fact that nature creates startling patterns – snowflakes, flowers, crystals and the like – so could electricity create these same effects in the fields? Lightning has struck the planet for millions of years, so this would have been a well-documented natural phenomenon. But in 1990 they were only just beginning to happen in other countries. Eighty per cent of the world's crop formations were occurring within an equilateral triangle, formed between Winchester, Warminster and Wantage. It also crossed my mind that there might be a connection between the crop formations and the abundance of archaeological sites within this triangle. Those and many other ideas passed through my mind as I looked for logical explanations. Early on, I began to conclude that this was a modern day phenomenon. However, it is now known that crop circles happened as far back as the year 1000 and by the 1600s they were thought to be made by corn devils.

As soon as I arrived home, I read the CPR pamphlet that the gentleman had given to me in the crop formation. It had Colin Andrews' telephone number on it, but when I rang the number all I got was an answering service. I tried several times later, but still had no luck. I had an overpowering feeling that I had to make contact with Colin Andrews, and it was not until about three weeks later that we first spoke (see picture section).

I read in a local newspaper that Colin and his colleague, Pat Delgado, would be in a local bookshop, signing a book they had written together called *Circular Evidence*. I thought that this would be a good time to touch base with Colin. But when I arrived at the shop, it was packed with people getting their books signed. Colin just had enough time to tell me that when he had finished his forthcoming tour of Australia, America and Japan, we could get together. So with a copy of their book tucked underneath my arm, I left. When I arrived home, I read their book from cover to cover, and it left no doubt in my mind of the authenticity of most crop formations at that time. It still left that big question though – what, or who, were the circle makers?

Weeks turned into months, and I was beginning to think that I would never see Colin again, let alone have a discussion. Then a friend visiting my home noticed a copy of *Circular Evidence* in my bookcase. He asked me if I was interested in the circle phenomenon. When he discovered I was, he told me that his son, Gary (Keel), and a friend of Gary's, James Withers, were active members of CPR, and had been gathering information all that season. They had also been present at Operation Blackbird, an all-night surveillance at Westbury, which was set up by Colin in association with the BBC and Nippon Television and at which the army had also been present.

I could not believe my luck. I asked him whether it would be possible to meet up with Gary, and the following week he rang me. He told me that there was to be a meeting at his home, and that I was welcome to come. Colin would also be there, he added. I waited in eager anticipation, knowing that I was about to learn more about the phenomenon.

By the time I arrived, Colin was already there, browsing through many of the diagrams that Gary and James had drawn up from the information they had gathered that season. Each crop formation was listed and given a grid reference. Each individual crop circle's floor pattern was also logged, so that Colin could feed all the information into his computer, making the information easy to retrieve at a later date. After this, we all relaxed and Colin began to tell us how he first became interested in crop formations.

In 1983 Colin was working as an electrical engineer for local government, and was returning from a job in Petersfield along the A272 towards Winchester. At Cheesefoot Head there is a natural amphitheatre called the Punchbowl. As Colin drove by, he happened to glance down, and what he saw changed his life. In the green corn, there was a quadruplet set of circles like those you would find on a dice. He was amazed at the sheer size and symmetry of this formation. Since that day, he said, he had personally photographed and measured over 1,000 of these formations. He had also logged over 3,000 into his computer. Until then I hadn't realised there were that many formations in existence. He told us the phenomena began as simple circles, but had developed into what were then called pictograms. He'd also heard about other strange phenomena happening in and around these formations.

In 1987 Colin received information that a lady walking her dogs in Kimpton, near Andover, had noticed some strange lights in the sky above a field. Colin went to investigate, and discovered a crop circle below where the lights had been seen. He took precise measurements as he had always done, but on returning home he discovered that he had missed one important measurement, and decided to return to the field that evening. He arrived just before dusk. After he had obtained the measurement, he stood in the crop formation for a moment. Although he's not a religious man, he put his hands together and prayed for some kind of help on the investigations into these circles, because after four years he was getting nowhere. As soon as he did this, a noise, something like a high pitched electronic buzz, came towards him from across the field. It stopped in a position close to him and began to increase in volume. He could tell its exact position and was beginning to panic. He then began to look for a point where he could exit the field as quickly as possible. But then it stopped. It seemed to sense that he was scared.

I asked Colin whether there was any scientific research

being carried out on the wheat itself. He told me that a laboratory in Stroud was using a new German method and had obtained some remarkable results. They say that every living thing has its own energy structures, and that by analysing certain samples of body tissue, by the energy they find they can tell the condition of the different organs of the body. Now because you can do this with any living thing they decided (out of idle curiosity) to put the wheat through the same procedure. They discovered that the actual crystalline structure had changed. It was as if a high energy had passed through the wheat. It seemed to me to be undeniable evidence that something out of the ordinary was occurring. This, if nothing else, deserved some attention from the government.

When the crop circles form early in the season the crop recuperates and tries to grow vertically as normal. When the corn is ripe it enters the food chain. Yet to our knowledge (at that point in time) the government was showing no interest whatsoever, even though there could have been a public health issue. Colin had asked the government for financial backing to help with the increasing cost of his research, but to no avail. Colin said, 'It was by pure chance the following year that I discovered a pilot had been paid for three months to fly over and film the crop formations by the Ministry of Agriculture. So we realised at that point that the government was showing a little interest in the crop formations.' However some members of the royal family have shown more than a little interest, and Colin had furnished them with as much information as he could on the whole phenomenon.

Then Colin told us a strange story that happened at his

home. He had converted his garage (which adjoins his house) into an office, and, because of the expensive equipment which he needed for his studies, he decided to install a security system. The system had worked fine, until one day he returned home with a soil sample from one of the circles. Because of the late hour, he decided to put the soil sample in the office and retire for the night. At 4.15am precisely the security alarm was activated. It woke the whole household. Thinking that the office had been broken into, Colin dashed down to investigate, but could find no reason for the alarm to have been activated. There were no visible signs of entry.

The next night at precisely 4.15am the alarm was activated again, and again it woke the whole house. Again Colin could find no reason for the alarm's activation. So the next day Colin phoned a friend who was also an electrical engineer. He asked his friend to check the system thoroughly, which he did, and still neither of them could find anything wrong. Then Colin asked his friend to build a system around that which was already installed. So within a few days both systems were operational. Between them they had designed a system which they felt was foolproof. Nothing could enter that building, be it through the ceiling, the floors, the walls, the doors, or the windows, without setting off the alarm. They felt it was impenetrable.

Nothing happened for about a week after they had secured the office. Then every night for two weeks at precisely 4.15am, the alarms were activated. You can imagine the kind of reaction it had on his family. They tried to persuade Colin to drop the whole investigation. However their anxiety passed, and Colin continued. These events were verified later by the police constable to whom Colin had reported the incidents.

It was at this point that I asked Colin whether any of the strange things that had happened to him over the years had affected his approach to the whole investigation. He told me that he tries to keep both feet firmly on the ground, and approach the whole operation as a scientific study, but sometimes things are so bizarre that it becomes very difficult.

'One morning I was sitting at my computer, logging in information on crop formations, when suddenly a voice, which was about an arm's length from my head and slightly to my right, said, "What are you doing?" It had a profound effect on me,' he said, 'and ultimately changed the way that I entered the data into the computer. How can you add something like that into a scientific study?'

He continued, 'I went to a crop formation the other day, and, when I arrived, there was a woman in the formation. I passed the time of day and proceeded to do my measuring. When I'd finished I began chatting to her. In the course of conversation she told me she was a medium, and that she'd been drawn to this particular formation. Then we began to talk generally, when all of a sudden she grabbed my arm very tightly with one hand and squeezed. Her eyes began to waver. "I have a message, I have a message coming through, it's for you, you've been chosen," she said. "You've been chosen to pick up a stone."' To save embarrassment and humour the woman, Colin looked around for a stone. There were literally thousands of them. It was a very stony part of the field. He looked for one particular stone and walked over to a spot where a stone was half buried in the soil. He wriggled it free from the dirt. As he turned it over there was a replica of the inner circle of Stonehenge on the other side (see picture section).

Pointing to his head, Colin said, 'I've learned to take everything on board, because you never know when it may become relevant to some other strange event.' Then Colin went on to say that while he was lecturing in Australia, he'd heard a story of a strange event which had happened at a dam, near West Turaff in the Mali region of Northwest Victoria. Colin went to investigate and spent a week at the farm of Nancy Jolly, on whose land the event took place.

Mr Jolly explained to Colin what happened on the evening of 6 December 1989: 'My son was sitting on the veranda and I was in the house, then suddenly my son called out, to draw my attention to what was happening above the dam. I quickly rushed outside and joined him on the veranda. For about five or ten minutes we both observed a yellowish-golden light hovering above the dam. Then suddenly it vanished. We noticed that all the time the light was over the dam, the sheep were very restless. It was a clear, starlit night so we decided to wait outside while the sheep settled down. At daybreak my son and I drove to the dam.' Mr Jolly went on, 'We couldn't comprehend what we saw next.'

Two thirds of the water in the dam had gone, and twelve crop circles had appeared in a field adjoining the dam. They were standard crop circles, four of them were twelve feet across, and the other eight ranged from between 6 and 8 feet in diameter. Three weeks later, sheep that were in a pen began to go frantic, and above them was another large yellow-orange light hovering over the pen. The night before Colin was due to leave the farm at the end of his week's stay, he drove up the old dirt road to take one last look at the dam and its surrounding area. He parked the car, switched off the headlights and got out. He closed the door behind him, and moved away from the car. It was then that he realised how much darker it was in the countryside in Australia than England. Fearing that he might lose sight of his car, he moved back to the driver's door and leant against it, letting his head roll back onto the roof.

He was then looking directly up into the night sky. He began thinking about a specific crop formation. He thought how nice it would be for a crop formation like this to appear in the fields near to where he was standing. A few days later a message was received at CPR headquarters back in England that a formation similar to the one Colin had thought about that night in Australia had appeared seven miles away from where he was stood. Coincidence? I wonder.

Colin then told us of a strange set of events that took place in 1976 just off the A272 where Colin had seen his first crop formation. It involved Joyce Bowls and Ted Pratt, who at the time were having an affair. They had parked a short distance along the Chilcombe Road, when Joyce and Ted saw a large golden ball of light appear over the field to their left. They watched it for a short time, when suddenly a shaft of light came from the underside of the hovering object.

Several alien beings walked through (not around) trees and bushes and surrounded their mini. One of the aliens leaned on the bonnet, and peered in at them. Needless to say they were both petrified. They were then taken aboard the craft. They were told and shown many things, some of which she believed she was not at liberty to divulge.

She did however contact Colin on the subject, because it involved Colin's work on the crop formations. Joyce told Colin that at one point the aliens had said, 'This is our field', indicating the field beneath. At the time it meant nothing to her, but when she became aware of Colin's work (and where the crop formations were occurring) she believed it might have some significance. When it was time to leave the craft they recalled very little.

The next thing they remembered was going around a round-about some 15 miles away on the outskirts of Southampton, which was not where they wanted to be. What makes this story believable is that they ruined both of their marriages to tell the media, because they felt it to be so important that the world knew.

Interestingly, the old megalithic yard is 2.72 feet, and when you realise the importance of the 'A' (a pyramidal shape) to our ancestors, is it more than a coincidence that Colin saw his first crop formation just off the A272? Or that Joyce Bowles and Ted Pratt had their close encounter of the third kind just off the A272? Since that time many crop formations have appeared in that field.

In 1990, Brian Tubb, an engineer whose job it is to mend combine harvesters, was called to a farm one mile from the A272. Combine harvesters do not usually break down at the farmyard, so he was following directions on an Ordnance Survey map. When he was getting close to the point where the harvester should be, he noticed a huge circle of flattened wheat in the same field. To make conversation, he commented about it to the farmer when he arrived. Brian was a sceptic at that time and said to the farmer, 'I see you have one of those hoaxes on your land.' The farmer replied, 'You think they're hoaxes do you?' The farmer asked Brian 'What time do you finish work?' Brian said 'About 5.30pm.' 'Stick around until 6.00pm and keep looking up,' said the farmer.

That evening Brian stopped work at 5.45pm and, intrigued, sat back on an embankment and looked up as the farmer had said. He told me that at around 6.00pm a flock of geese flew over the field. Being a countryman himself, he could not believe what he saw next.

He knew that geese fly in a direct course when returning from where they feed to their roosting site, and maintain a V-shaped flying formation. As the geese neared the circle they broke formation, flew around the crop circle and regrouped once they reached the other side. This was my first clue that the magnetic field may be disturbed in and above a crop formation.

The only strange story I could think of to go with this bevy of information was one that I experienced on 1 June 1974. I had the TV on in the lounge and was not taking too much notice of it, until what appeared to be a news bulletin came on at around 10 to 1. A gentleman in a trenchcoat was standing some distance away from a chemical plant that was on fire behind him. In the foreground just behind him were firemen who seemed to be a long way from the actual fire to be of any use in putting it out. As he spoke, it became obvious why. The fire, he claimed, was so hot it was melting windows half a mile away.

Given the temperature required to melt glass, it must have been impossible to get anywhere near that fire for hours.

These details stuck in my mind so much so that when my wife returned from shopping around 3 o'clock I told her of the event. When it came time for the 6 o'clock news, I called my wife into the lounge to see it for herself. The newsreader said, 'At around 4.45pm today, a huge fire broke out at a chemical plant at Flixborough and firemen from several fire brigades in that area are trying to bring it under control.' Then he said, 'We are now going over live to Flixborough.' To my amazement it was exactly the same report that I had seen at 10 to 1. My wife said, 'How did you see this before it happened?' All I could say was that I had.

At a later date, Arthur C Clarke investigated the phenomenon because several other people had also seen it at the same time as me. At the time I was not into premonitions, so I looked for a logical answer. The report would have been bounced via satellite to our TV sets through the equipment at the TV centre, so it would have gone into space and back. What could possibly have sent it back to four hours before it happened? Several people saw it, so it did happen, but how?

We sat there listening to story after story and I remember wondering where the hell it was all leading. The meeting finally wound up at around midnight, and since that night Colin has become a great friend, as have Gary and James and their families. When I arrived home I found it very difficult to sleep, and at 2.00am found myself wandering around the house trying to formulate logical answers to and explanations for all that I'd heard that evening. I thought it was impossible. These were genuine guys telling me what they considered to be genuine stories. So to get logical answers for illogical stories, I allowed myself the luxury of believing that everything I'd heard was accurate and true. I then tried to imagine the whole concept from an extra-terrestrial point of view.

Some people think that if there are such things as extra-terrestrial beings (that have travelled thousands of light years across the universe from a distant star system) they would automatically land outside the Houses of Parliament, or the White House and say, 'Hi, we're your new neighbours!' It's this very earthly, almost Neanderthal, way of thinking that has wiped out almost all of the indigenous peoples of our planet. 'Hi, we're your new neighbours, we've got it right, you've got it wrong. From now on you do it our way, because if you don't we have the power to wipe you out, and will do so without hesitation. You've got no one on your side, we have God on ours. So sit down, don't moan, be quiet, don't argue, and we'll get along fine together. Oh and by the way, your country now belongs to us. Have a nice day.'

Even at this level of thinking (that of our ancestors), unless aliens had done some investigative work, they could just as easily land in Tiananmen Square on a bad day, or outside a civic hall in Bosnia, or Baghdad. Do you get the picture? Have you noticed that it has become increasingly difficult to find somewhere safe to go on holiday? It's about time you realised, if you hadn't already, that we are a very barbaric race. I'm sure that someone with the intelligence to travel thousands of light years across the universe is not going to land willy nilly somewhere on our planet and be blown away by some crazies.

Let's imagine for a while that, in the star system Orion, there is a planet that cooled from its molten state 20 million years before the Earth, and that life itself began 20 million years before that of the Earth. Evolving at the same rate as ours, it would be logical to think that the life forms could be 20 million years more advanced than our own civilisations here on Earth. Try to imagine that they reached the same point in their evolution as we've reached today, 20 million years ago. Let's also imagine that they were able to conquer disease, poverty, pollution, wars and, finally, 20 million years ago they launched into space, and have since conquered light travel, time travel and forms of travel that we could not even conceive today. I'm sure that their brilliant minds would have needed the stimulation to travel through space and seek out other civilisations of the same intelligence that they themselves possess.

Here on Earth we are just beginning to realise the stupidity of enforcing our particular culture's beliefs and ways of life onto people from other walks of life. Any government with any grey matter between its ears would know that this is wrong. But it still happens.

Let's also imagine that these beings crossed space and time and discovered the existence of Earth eight million years ago or more (and I suspect more) and compared to their level of intelligence we seemed so backward that they just observed us from a safe distance and have done so ever since. They would also have seen our recent primitive attempts to explore space before we'd solved the problems we have on Earth. They might believe that we have reached a point in our evolution where it is possible to give us a helping hand into the future that we so desperately seek.

Over that eight million years, might they have helped us indirectly? Could they have observed us rolling heavy stones on logs, and helped us to invent the wheel? Might they have looked over our shoulder 4,000 years ago and helped us to invent the plough, which gave mankind more time to develop his arts and his culture? Could it be that 2,000 years ago they even helped with the birth of Christianity, and the belief in one God and – dare I say it – even have been there and had something to do with the birth of Jesus? What was the bright star over Bethlehem? Could this have all been done to bring mankind together, to make him think as one? Could they still be looking over our shoulder now, in the present day, and can they see that religion is now fragmenting and pulling mankind apart? Could they know that this would and should happen before we can really break through to the new age? I believe that, since the birth of Christ, we have again reached a critical point in the evolution of mankind – a turning point.

The human race has been taught for 2,000 years to follow in the footsteps of God, and if mankind doesn't understand right from wrong by now, when will he? Is there going to be a point where we can put what we've learnt from Christianity into practice? There should be, but I think not. This is how I was thinking that night in late 1990. My thoughts today have changed on those subjects – but not by that much.

CHAPTER 3

It wasn't a hard winter that year, but it seemed to go on and on, and to make the time pass more quickly I became engrossed in writing songs for our new album. I normally start this procedure by treating myself to a brand new notepad and pen. So about 10 o'clock one evening while the family were watching TV, I slipped quietly away into my den to begin. I sat at the desk and opened the pad, I put pen to paper, and then something happened which has never happened to me before or since.

Immediately and without thinking I began to write, and I found myself looking at the end of the pen to see what I was writing. I don't quite know how to explain the feelings that I had when I read through what I had just written, but it prompted me to phone Colin and tell him. I knew it wasn't a song, and I had never written poetry before, but it was a poem.

I just told Colin that something strange had happened, and he informed me that his new video had turned up that day, so we arranged to meet at 10.30am the next morning at his house.

By the time I arrived, Colin had set up his video, and after a few verbal pleasantries and a handshake, we sat down to watch the video. When the video was about half way through, I reached into my pocket and gave Colin the poem, because the words he was using in his video were in my poem. We looked at one another in absolute amazement. We could not believe that what Colin was saying in his video, was there in the words of my poem. I called the poem *Mother Earth – The Truth*, and it goes as follows:

In the Summer 1990, when the heat was quite intense,
I draw to your attention, a chain of strange events,
Things have happened to me, and to some of my
best friends,
A phenomenon is happening, and the mystery never ends.

I remember reading somewhere, of a circle in the corn,
It appeared due west of where I live, and just before
the dawn.
A compelling feeling told me, that I really had to go,
So I left home fairly quickly, and drove 40 miles or so.

As I reached the Vale of Pewsey, and the White Horse
on the hill,
The sight I saw beneath me gave my bones a sudden chill.
There stretched out below me, 60 metres down the field,

A pictogram of many shapes, what secrets would it yield?
Since then I've seen so many, and walked in quite a few,
And I've the strangest feeling, that the patterns hold
the clue.
I've heard so many answers, from folks who think
they know,
But the truth to this enigma unfolds very, very slow.

You must draw on all conclusions, and don't laugh
at anyone,
Cause the answer is in all of us, who live beneath the Sun.
Our Mother has a problem, and a problem we have made,
And She tries to tell us slowly, in the corn She gently lays.

Younger brothers do not listen, and the time is getting
short,
So Mother has to frighten us, but as a last resort,
She'll conjure up the evil winds, that will move the
Seven Seas,
And move the molten mountains, and bring countries
to their knees.

Then we shall see a vision, like the world has never seen,
Something will come with light and sound, to end our
nightmare dream.
From that day on the world will change, in every way
we know,
And those that come will help us all, to make the whole
world grow.

So little men of power, who never got things right,
And are probably laughing at this now, will get the
biggest fright.
Your money will mean nothing, and power's not the key,
The answer's simply balance, and perfect harmony.

Now I'm sure that all those words must have been in my mind
ready to come out, but it was the way that it happened and the
timing of how it happened. For Colin's video to have been
ready that next day, and for us both to sit there and see the use
of those words may have been a wild coincidence. I wonder.

Over the coming weeks and months Colin and I met on a
regular basis, and our friendship has grown to the point where
we can confide in one another about some highly classified
information, and know that it won't be in the daily newspaper
the following day. I must also say that I would not divulge any
information without Colin's prior knowledge and vice versa.
We both feel that when the time is right things should be said,
so that more people can understand what is actually going on.
It has also crossed my mind that this may be the way that
governments are thinking: 'When the time is right.' We can
only hope.

In July 1989, Colin and Pat Delgado were invited to go on a
morning TV programme at Pebble Mill, Birmingham, to talk
about an experience they shared at Beckhampton. They were in
a formation, being filmed by a BBC television crew, and heard
and recorded a strange, high-pitched buzzing sound – the same
sound Colin had heard at Kimpton. The cameraman had also
experienced total camera failure while this noise was present,

which cost the cameraman a fortune to put right.

They had just booked into a hotel when they received a call from the producer, David Morgaston, who told them they had received a letter from a man in Scotland called Sandy Reed, who claimed that he saw a crop circle form early one morning. David Morgaston asked Pat and Colin if they could think of any questions that he could ask this man to find out the validity of his claim, which they did. The outcome was that the man was invited down to the show, and placed amongst the audience.

When the appropriate time came, the host introduced the man, saying that he was doing some research on foxes in the early hours of the morning when he saw a crop circle form in a field near Dundee. He spoke for a few minutes on what actually happened and Colin thought that was the end of it. A few weeks later, Colin was asked to do another TV show in East Anglia, and while he was on, he noticed that this man was in the audience again. Everything up to this point was normal, the man had seen a crop circle form, and he had a right to be there. Nothing was out of the ordinary until, that is, one evening at the end of the crop formation season, when Colin received a knock on his door at about 10.30pm.

When Colin opened the door he recognised the man immediately as the one at the two TV shows, the man that had seen the crop circles form. Colin was surprised this man was knocking on his door at such a late hour. He told Colin that he had something very important to tell him and Pat Delgado, and that Colin should ring Pat and tell him to come over immediately.

When Pat arrived, the man began asking them questions, and it got to the point where they were wondering when he was going to get to the point, and tell them what was so important. But he just kept on asking them questions. When he'd asked a question of one of them, he'd look at the face of the other to see their reaction. Colin said it was strange that he should even be there, because he wasn't saying anything that we didn't already know, and he was asking all the questions.

Pat became impatient and said, 'If you've nothing further to say or add, I must leave', trying to force the man to say what he'd come for. But he didn't, and Pat left. Then the man suggested that he and Colin should take a walk, so Colin put on his coat and they walked out of the door and down the road, with the man asking question after question. They walked up and down the road three or four times, and as they approached Colin's home for the fourth time Colin said, 'I really must go in now'. The man told Colin to get the keys to his car; they were going for a drive. The man had a domineering, menacing attitude. Colin thought that if there was going to be any trouble, then maybe he should be away from the house, because his wife and family were inside.

So Colin did no more than get his keys, start the car, and drive off into the night with this stranger. The man asked Colin where the nearest crop formation was, and Colin told him it was near Winchester. The man said, 'Take me there.' By now it was about 12.30am. Colin found himself standing in a field, in a crop formation, talking to a man he hardly knew. His Scottish accent became very pronounced, and Colin sensed that he was about to tell him something.

What the man told Colin put him in fear of his life. He told Colin that he was from the CIA, and that from now on Colin would take orders from him, and him alone. When Colin was asked to do TV or radio he would be instructed what to say. He was also told that from then on he would have to buy two newspapers, and that he would get instructions in code through these papers. The man said to Colin, 'You are now one of us.' He would set up a bank account in Switzerland that would finance all Colin's research into the phenomenon. But for this he would have to do exactly what he was told.

Colin didn't agree to anything, but listened to what the man had to say. Colin thought that this nightmare would soon be over when the man ushered him back to the car, but it wasn't to be. As they turned onto the main road and came to an intersection, Colin went to turn right back to Andover and his home; the man said, 'Take a left, we're going to Southampton.' Colin did as he was told and within half an hour they were parking outside a block of apartments in Shirley, near Southampton. The man ushered Colin out of the car and towards the main door. A girl of about 18 or 19 passed behind the door and pushed a button, the door opened. The man did not acknowledge the girl. Colin was ushered into a lift and taken to the tenth floor. The man rang the bell but nobody came, he rang again and again but nobody came. He looked through the letterbox and shouted a name, but still nobody came. He seemed to be angry, and was getting more so. At that point Colin was allowed to go home.

Colin was worried sick for days afterwards thinking about what the man could do if Colin didn't agree to what was said.

As luck would have it Colin remembered that a friend of his had joined the police force many years ago and had become a high-ranking man in MI5. Colin rang him and told him the whole story. His friend said that the CIA had no jurisdiction in our country and to ignore everything that he had been told. Colin did ignore him, although the CIA man tried to make contact on many other occasions, and that seemed to be an end to the matter.

At this point I began to wonder what I was getting myself into, from a simple crop formation in a field to the CIA! Was there more to this than met the eye. Why the CIA? Was there a cover-up going on? If so, a cover-up of what? If, as the papers were saying at the time, these crop circles were all hoaxes, why were the CIA so interested in this phenomenon? Question after question.

I couldn't wait for the new season of crop formations to begin, so that I could start my own investigations into these phenomena. I thought it was best that I should treat myself to an early birthday present. So in early May 1991, I bought myself a camcorder. I didn't have to wait very long to put it to good use. Around the middle of May, I received a phone call from James Withers who told me there was a crop formation at Sutton Scotney in a field of oil seed rape. He believed it to be the first of the season. So I loaded my camcorder and headed off towards Sutton Scotney.

After walking through a small field we came across a rather large circle about 25 metres across. The rape was flattened to the ground, and most of the stems were bent. I couldn't believe that the stems were actually bent and not broken (see picture section). What could bend something that is as thick as your middle finger and not break it? I did a little experiment. I walked to the edge of the circle, and from some of the standing rape plants, I chose one section to push down to see if it would bend. As I applied weight to it, it immediately snapped at the base. What did this? I was both puzzled and excited. Here, I thought, was a real mystery.

I soon realised that we had to get to these crop formations soon after they were formed, before too many feet had trampled in and out of them. In the coming months we were able to do this with the help of pilots and farmers who would phone in to the CPR headquarters as soon as they spotted a formation. We were able, through June and July, to film and measure most of the crop formations in a 40-mile radius of our hometown of Andover (see picture section).

As we entered each crop formation, we automatically walked over to the edge to discover if the stems of the crop inside the formation were bent or broken. This, we believed, could tell us if the formation was genuine or not.

When too many people have walked in the crop formation it eventually breaks the stems, but you can still see the floor patterns of the formation. Also, with the help of the divining rods we can sense the different energies found in the crop formation.

Later that year, our attention was brought to a formation that had appeared in Litchfield, near Whitchurch. This formation was one of many that were being called 'insectograms' because of their resemblance to insects. Doug and Dave (the notorious hoaxers) were saying they created it, and they probably did. It was very messy. The strange thing is when we entered the crop formation, we noticed that at one end there was a ladder effect at the back of a D-shaped section. The ladder effect was splayed, and each individual strut gave off a different kind of energy in opposite directions. This changed when we went back a day later. We still haven't been able to fathom this out. So if this was man-made as Doug and Dave claim, who changed the energies?

In July that year, Colin had organised an operation called Black Swan, at Adams Grave just north of Eastfield at Alton Barnes. I was invited to go along but, because of a heavy workload with the Troggs, I only managed to get there for one long afternoon. When I arrived, Gary Keel and his mother were sitting in chairs outside a caravan at the top of Adams Grave, looking out over the fields. There were already three crop formations in the fields below, and Gary had brought along the powerful telescope that he uses for astronomy.

I arrived around midday, and at approximately half past one Gary drew my attention to the horizon, which must have been 20 to 25 miles away. I had my binoculars with me, and we both peered at the distant horizon. Gary pointed out that there was something hovering about an inch to an inch and a half above the horizon. I couldn't make it out with my binoculars, so I took a look through his telescope. We could not make out exactly what it was, but it was an elliptical shape, and very, very faint. We both watched this off and on for the next 25 minutes, before it suddenly disappeared.

There are many military and air force bases in this area and it was not unusual to see helicopters. We took it to be one of these, although helicopters don't usually hover for 25 minutes, and simply logged the event.

It's peculiar how the human mind reacts to strange events that it can't quite grasp. This brings me to something that happened to Gary two days later. It was around 11 o'clock at night when Gary decided to take a walk around the caravan where the surveillance equipment was kept. He reached the end of the caravan where the tow bar protrudes and as he went to move around the corner he said, 'I was stopped by an invisible wall of what I can only describe as energy.' It made every hair on his body stand on end.

What he didn't do was to look directly up, because days later some villagers told us that, at 11 o'clock on that same night they saw a triangular shape hovering above the caravan. Gary had thought that he was having a funny turn, not that something was causing him to feel the way he did. If it hadn't been for me asking Gary if anything had occurred on that watch, I believe he would have forgotten all about it. But it seemed to jog something in his sub-conscious mind, and he woke up to the fact that something had happened. Was he meant to forget?

One evening later that month, I received a telephone call from James, who told me that Gary had managed to acquire some amazing footage of some strange events that happened in fields in and around Alton Barnes. Some of the events were captured on film by Nippon Television, but the footage that amazed me most was filmed by crop circle enthusiast Steven Alexander and his wife.

They were out filming a formation at Milk Hill near Alton

Barnes and were just about to leave the area when, out of the corner of her eye, his wife noticed something dancing around in the corn. He panned his camera across and filmed an object approximately 9 inches in diameter – about the size of a football – sniffing erratically around, in, and above the corn, like a dog. It amazed me to see this object actually roaming around at will. It wasn't being blown in the wind!

There was no noise whatsoever and it seemed to be looking for something. It moved around in one spot for about 30 or 40 seconds, and then moved directly across the field in a straight line to another area and searched that. Then it went back to its original position back across the field. It did this several times.

Then suddenly it shot up the field at what I would estimate to be about 60 mph at the height of the corn, over a hedgerow then over some trees. It then passed behind a tractor. As the tractor driver was nearing the end of the field he turned and noticed the ball going up the field. It seemed to disappear into the ground in places, then it jumped over a ridge, and when it finally arrived at the crest of the hill, it went up into the sky and disappeared.

Later the tractor driver was asked what he saw, and he described what Steven Alexander and his wife had filmed. The farmer told his workmates, who ridiculed him, so he decided to keep quiet about it. However, he became rather excited when he discovered that someone else had seen and filmed the same object. He then began to talk openly about it.

Gary and James also had footage of the inaugural flight of Concorde. In this piece of footage a ball very similar to the one that was filmed by Steven Alexander passes down the front edge wing of Concorde. It goes below the aircraft, then back up, appears to look in four windows, and then disappears up into the sky. How could that be possible if Concorde was travelling at 6/700 miles an hour?

The Nippon TV coverage was also very strange. It showed a swirling mass about 150 ft above the land, and they were able to zoom in close. The lines that make up a TV picture could not keep up with the speed at which this object was oscillating and spinning on its axis. The object itself was blurred, however nothing else in the frame was. Nippon TV had carried out some enhancement on the film. They put each individual frame down as a plate, then enhanced each one and put them back into position. What then appeared was similar to the nose cone of a rocket, but upside down. In the lower nose part of the object there was a ball coming out, which can be seen in one of the frames.

When I eventually acquired this film myself, I slowed it down to one frame at a time, and noticed that there were several ball like objects dropping out of the bottom of this craft. They appeared to be the same objects that were seen and filmed at Milk Hill and in the Concorde footage. All of these films were shot in broad daylight and I have acquired copies of them and subsequently many others.

As I explained at the beginning of the book, governments world-wide have been able to keep a lot of these things from us, but with the help of the camcorder it is just a matter of time before we get something very interesting and unbelievable on film. The more of these strange phenomena that you see captured on film by other people, the more you want to experience them yourself. I had to wait another year before I was to have that pleasure.

As 1991 marched on, it became apparent that more people worldwide were becoming interested in the crop formations. Apart from Japanese, American, German and BBC television, many other nationalities were turning up from all across the world trying to get something on film. Some of the media became very impatient, and throughout 1991 began to make their own crop formations so they would get some kind of story for their programmes. They were inviting crop investigators to talk about the crop circles that they themselves had made, but told the crop investigators that they had appeared overnight and pretended they knew nothing about them. At first glance two of the investigators thought one of these formations was genuine, and the media had a 'field' day.

What was desperately needed was a foolproof method by which investigators could walk into the formation and know immediately if it was real or a hoax. This was finally achieved, and we now have the technology to do this.

What the media failed to realise was that investigators are (on the whole) ordinary people with a limited income, and it takes quite a while for them to build up enough resources to buy the technology needed to prove that the circles are genuine. But this is now happening.

Throughout that season many different kinds of formations were occurring in many of the usual areas. One in particular formed at Stonehenge. It was an insectogram. Doug and Dave the hoaxers had called the press and TV cameras to the field to prove they had made this particular formation. They said,

'Look we even signed it!' There were two Ds in the formation which they said stood for Doug and Dave. But amazingly, when an aerial photograph was taken of the formation, in the bottom left hand corner of the picture was another insectogram exactly the same shape as the one in the ripened corn, which Doug and Dave knew nothing about! It must have been laid down earlier in the season and missed by the aerial spotters. This information begs the question, Who is pulling the strings? Who are the circle makers? (See picture section).

Some days James, Gary and myself would travel over a hundred miles in a round trip, trying to photograph and measure all of the different formations, which took most of our spare time. It is well known that at the end of the crop formation season there is the mother of all crop formations, and 1991 was no exception. Two formations had formed. One in Cambridge, and one at Barbury Castle (see picture section). The formation in Cambridge was a replica of the Mandelbrot set.

The Mandelbrot set is the graph of a mathematical formula. It takes its name from Benoit Mandelbrot, the mathematician who first fed the formula into a computer. Dr Mandelbrot was also the first to use the term 'fractal', from the Latin *fractus* meaning 'to break'. The Mandelbrot set has been called the most complex known mathematical object. It is one of a class of formulae that create simple shapes, which grow more complex as the shape is repeated in miniature around the edges of the first shape. Still smaller versions of the shape grow out of these smaller shapes and so on to infinity. The result is a field of infinite, swirling complexity.

One part of this fascinating kind of mathematics is that it looks as if this might be how nature operates. As you explore the Mandelbrot set you run into all sorts of seemingly organic shapes. Twig, leaf, flower, fish, seed and branch shapes are everywhere and they are often arranged in the midst of flows like air and water. Likewise if you explore nature you run into all kinds of fractal shapes. The repetition of shapes and angles at every scale is everywhere. Fractal geometry seems to be able to describe the kinds of shapes that actually occur in our organic world.

The aerial shot of the Mandelbrot set really got me thinking. When I was at college we were taught how to draw and construct five-centred arches of the kind you may find above church windows. (See picture section).

Because of this training, I looked at the Mandelbrot set to see how it was constructed. The major shape is like a heart, as seen in the diagram. This can only be drawn by using seven centres, marked here by the crosses. But, as you see in the aerial picture, the whole pattern is laid down from one point. This is impossible.

At the end of July when the corn was still green, we were told of a huge configuration at Barbury Castle near Swindon. We managed to track it down, and when I saw the scale of this formation, no one could have conceivably made it from the ground. It was much too complex. It was overwhelmingly tetrahedral, and although I didn't realise at the time, a year later we would find out just how important this configuration was.

It was during 1991 that scientists were beginning to wake up to the fact that we had a genuine phenomenon on our hands, and it was at this time that physicists and scientists began to get interested. Although they still didn't become involved by name, they were interested enough for Colin to be able to send many of his diagrams over to the States, and by the end of 1991 there was some interesting information filtering slowly back from America.

One physicist in particular that I'm not allowed to name had discovered that because the circles that Colin had sent weren't accurate circles (they were slightly elongated) it made more sense to him than if they had been perfect circles. He was able to tell us that each circle would make a different tone, and that the circles that Colin had sent across were the white notes of a piano keyboard. However, the 'A' was missing, and at the time this left us wondering what kind of a message this actually was, if any at all. There always seemed to be lots of questions and not very many answers.

By the end of 1991, I was paying attention to the whole design rather than the floor patterns. It was similar to looking at a painting rather than its brush strokes, and it seemed likely that if a UFO were to leave a message it would be in the form of an overall design.

I was becoming fully aware of the coincidences that had been occurring. There was the compulsive feeling that I had to go to the first crop circle, the man with the crash helmet who had the information I needed to find Colin's telephone number, Colin's book in the bookcase that somebody else noticed so that I could get to meet Colin, the poem that was finished the day Colin's video arrived, the same wording, the same message. Just small things, that lock themselves away in your subconscious mind. Little did I know that they would lead to bigger things! I felt that there must be a reason for my involvement in these phenomena. And the urge to know more drove me on. We all met several times over the winter that year and little snippets of information were passed around. We were all left wondering what surprises the new season would have in store for us.

CHAPTER 4

I had already made up my mind that in 1992 I would devote more of my time to the study of these phenomena. I was also to find out that year how important it is to have a liaison with the local police. One of the first crop circles which formed in late May was again in Sutton Scotney, close to where a formation had occurred the previous year. It was immediately assumed by a television crew to be a hoax because all the stems of the plants were broken, but the television company was unaware that over 16 people had already walked in it.

I had been into that formation days before they even arrived with their cameras. The formation itself was about 25 feet across. The central core of the formation was made up of a tight swirl of around 5 feet in diameter that coiled around on itself. Ninety per cent of the crop of rape was bent, not broken. You cannot bend rape, it snaps like celery. So what made them think it was a hoax?

One local investigator claimed that the police were contacted by two coach-loads of people who were leaving the service station just south of Bullington Cross. It was also claimed that they told the police they had seen a large orange-golden light directly above the field where the formation appeared. It was suggested that it was very similar to an orange or golden light that the army had filmed on a watch in 1990. It immediately made me think, Those lucky devils – or words to that effect. It made me hope that one day I would be in the right place at the right time to see or film my own sighting.

However, after checking this out with the CPR police contact, no such report was made on the evening in question. This proved to me how careful you have to be to check all information. The investigator who was responsible for this information was already under our watchful eye, because of other unreliable information she had given us. Some people are definitely in it for their 15 minutes of fame. This is exactly how mis- or disinformation works – it becomes so muddled that no one believes anything.

At our next meeting, Colin told me about a strange event that had taken place in Switzerland. A farmer walked onto his land and discovered a hole had appeared overnight in solid rock. It was 32 metres deep, as large as a house and had not one scrap of dirt or debris in the bottom. Had I not seen the photographs it would have been hard to believe. Over the year the numbers of that particular phenomenon had risen to seven.

I also heard of a similar event that took place on the French/Belgian border, again overnight. It was a crop-type formation but in the soil, and was around a metre deep. On 28 May I was the first person to see a crop formation just south of Andover at Cowdown whilst returning from Heathrow in a coach. It gave me great pleasure to be able to phone up the CPR and tell them something that for the first time they didn't already know.

In early July, Colin, Busty and I decided to fly over some of the early circles. Although visibility was poor on the morning that we chose to fly, we did pass over an interesting formation that had appeared at Chilbolton. Two strange things were supposed to have happened above the field where this circle had formed. A hang-glider went out of control and crashed into it. The hang-glider pilot said there was no obvious reason for the accident. A week later a balloonist was forced across the field, against the wind. Both of them had no explanation for what had happened, but one or two pilots of light aircraft have encountered downward forces working on their aircraft while circling this formation.

On returning to the airfield at Thruxton we stopped off for breakfast in the canteen. A television crew was waiting, and Colin and myself were asked if we would go over to Beckhampton to be interviewed, because several new formations had appeared. We agreed, and on the way over Colin informed me that he'd arranged with Tim and Polly Carson – a local farmer and his wife – to hold a secret watch on their land at Woodborough Hill, Alton Barnes, between 20–30 July. You get a 360-degree view from that particular hill. It is a very good position. Colin also told me that there would be several other bodies of investigators there. That part of the investigation would be run by Dr Steven Greer from America.

I arrived in the afternoon of 20 July in a deluge of rain. It rained all afternoon and on into the evening, and the first day was an absolute washout. The following day, people were already beginning to gather on top of the hill as I arrived, and by nightfall there were well over a hundred people. They had field glasses, cameras, video recorders, telescopes, night sights, anything that would peer into the night sky. A lot of people, I thought, for a so-called secret operation. But there was no need to worry, because as the night went on the people became fewer, and as the days went by the numbers dropped even further. At the beginning of an average evening there were between 30 and 50 people on the hill, which by 2.00am had sometimes dropped to as few as ten. I'll never forget that first evening because anything that moved was photographed! Anything that was in the sky was oohed and aahed at as if it were a fireworks display. People expected something to happen immediately for them, and it wasn't going to be that way.

At around 11 o'clock that night, the RAF at Upavon gave us an almighty show of flares. Dozens in the sky at one time, but as the nights went on we realised that at 11.30pm it all stopped, and we imagined them going back to their base for cocoa. War was over, for that evening.

I had a strange feeling that something was going to happen, for whatever reason, on 24 July, and I began telling people about this feeling. On the night of the 22nd, and into the early hours of the morning, heavy dew came upon the hill, and most of the equipment including the camcorders was covered with water. People dashed to put cameras away, and for the rest of the evening we just used our eyes and our binoculars to scour the skies. On the evening of 23 July, I was the only one brave enough to set up my camcorder. All the others remembered the previous evening with the heavy dew.

I was talking to Colin and one of his colleagues, Lynda Howes from America, and standing about 20 feet from my camera. She was telling an interesting story that occurred in New York. Two CIA agents were driving through New York with the Secretary General of the UN, Javier Perez de Cuellar, in the back seat. The time was 4.15 am. They had stopped at a set of traffic lights; one of the CIA agents noticed an orange-golden elliptical shape in the sky, and their first reaction was to think that the sun was rising, but then they realised the time.

The light appeared above a 12-storey block of apartments, then slowly moved out over the front of the building above the street, and then down two storeys to the tenth floor. One of them grabbed some field glasses out of the glove box and began to watch what was occurring. For a few moments the orange light remained stationary outside of a tenth floor apartment, then suddenly three beams of white tubular light came from the object, and shone through the tenth floor window.

Then two small balls, about 9 inches in diameter, began to travel along the beams of light. As they moved forward they went directly through the glass. At this point one of the CIA men dashed up to the tenth floor, to check the number of the apartment. Meanwhile, back in the street, three objects came back through the window. The middle object, according to the CIA man looking through his binoculars, was a woman in the foetus position, in her nightclothes. The two lights on either side of her opened up and appeared to be two humanoids. She was passed a small orange globe which disappeared into her. They all then changed into three white 9-inch spheres of light and disappeared into the large elliptical orange light.

As they watched a beam of light came down into their car, Perez De Cuellar was taken into the light and disappeared into the orange object. The whole orange object then dived into the East River. The two CIA men were stunned by what they'd witnessed, but quickly regained their composure and phoned their base. A call was put out to every police station in the area to be on the lookout for anything that seemed out of the ordinary.

Two hours had gone by when one of the police stations near the dock phoned the CIA headquarters and reported that they'd picked up a woman in her nightclothes, and Perez De Cuellar, walking along the dock. They were both bewildered and unaware of what had happened to them and that two hours had passed. The CIA men asked the police to tell them where the woman lived, and she gave her address as the same one where they had witnessed this entire happening. Nine other people also reported that they had seen a strange orange light in the sky (which had then dived into the East

River) all from vantage points that the CIA men knew to be in the area, including other apartments and bridges.

I've heard that Perez De Cuellar had a nervous breakdown, or that he is in a mental institution, but nobody seems to know for sure what happened to him. It is strange though how he disappeared off the scene so suddenly. I fired a few questions at Lynda, like 'What do they think the orange light was that they passed into the woman in those beams?' Many surmise that they are surveillance pods. If the entities want to survey someone, they'll find somebody close to them, and hand them one of these pods. The pod is then released at a later time in the house of the person they wish to survey.

Now you may think that this is far-fetched as I did, but where is Perez De Cuellar? Why did he disappear so suddenly? One other thing that I noticed in Lynda's account was the time that the CIA men reported this phenomenon as occurring – 4.15am. The same time that Colin's security system had been activated for those two weeks. Coincidence? I think not.

As we stood there talking, I glanced over Colin's shoulder to the west and I saw what I first thought was an aircraft light. It was low in the sky, about the same brightness as a star, and moving from left to right – south to north. I drew Colin and Lynda's attention to it, and then we all suddenly realised that it wasn't a plane. We watched it for a few seconds, and then I dashed over to my camcorder and switched it on.

As I looked through the eyepiece, it was then that I noticed the date and time – 24 July, 12:33am. It was the date I'd been telling everyone about, the date on which I felt something was going to happen. I filmed the object for about three and a half minutes, and had to move my camera twice to keep up with it as it slowly moved from south to north across the valley.

It was as bright as a star, but unlike a star it slowly kept dipping in brightness. It did this continuously across the valley, until it reached a certain point on the other side. It looked as if it was going to go out altogether, when all of a sudden it became four or five times brighter than a star and changed to a golden ball. It stayed motionless for about three minutes, and appeared to be slowly oscillating.

There were between 30 and 50 people on the hill that night, and nobody could come up with an explanation for what it was. It always seems easier to ask what it is not. It was not a plane, it was not a helicopter, it was not a flare, and it made no noise. It is not unusual when you see something in the sky just to look at the object. On a watch, we try to make contact if possible. I flashed my torch six times in succession at it as it crossed the valley, but with no response.

The second time I used my torch to signal it, the object immediately dropped in light intensity and size, and became the size of a white star again. Then, very quickly, it moved farther north, losing light intensity before vanishing. As I was searching for the last embers of light from the object through the viewfinder, others on the hill had noticed a white light shooting up into the sky suddenly splitting into a red and a white light, still heading in a northerly direction, but almost directly upwards. Because I was looking through the viewfinder I missed this event entirely.

A few days later it was discovered that someone else on the

watch in another area was looking at the same object through night sights, and could see the object rotating in an anti-clockwise direction. This probably appeared to me as oscillation. No one was able to capture anything better than this on film. But three nights later, at around 11 o'clock on the evening of the 27th, two people noticed two large shapes of light on the corn. It was as if someone were shining a torch at it, but there was no beam.

Then, at 5 past 12 in the early hours of the 28th, there began a heavy drizzle which became harder at about 10 past 12. People began to move off Woodborough Hill and down towards their cars, which were parked behind the barn at the foot of the hill.

My daughter had taken my place on the watch for two evenings, because I had commitments in Germany. She arrived at her car at around 12.20am. It was raining more heavily by then, and people were leaving quickly. Karen was saying goodnight to the CPR team, who were spending the whole ten days in a caravan parked behind the barn. A few seconds earlier, Colin had said his goodbyes and was making his way in his car along the concrete farm track.

Suddenly, those that were left heard an electronic buzzing type of sound, which got louder and louder. Then as suddenly as it came, it stopped. Karen looked across and saw that Colin's car had stopped in a lay-by on the concrete road, and thought that he had also heard the sound. But it turned out that Colin was just making sure that he had all his belongings with him, and was unaware of what had just happened. This all happened within a minute or so.

Karen said her goodbyes to the CPR team again, and went to sit in her car. She waited for a few more minutes chatting with her friend Susan, who had joined her on this particular watch. They were both exited about what they had just witnessed but couldn't understand it. Then Karen noticed Colin pulling away and followed him off the site.

Meanwhile, Dr Steven Greer, who had been doing an experiment on Remote Viewing in a circle to the north, at the foot of Woodborough Hill, with two other people – a woman from Holland and an English archaeologist – was leaving along another old farm track. This linked up with the concrete road where my daughter and Colin had just left in their cars. But instead of turning right and following them out, Steven Greer decided to go left and parked at the same place that Colin had, but facing in the opposite direction.

From the window of their car they peered out and saw a light very near the canal. He said it couldn't have been more than 500 yards away. Then suddenly the single light turned into what he described as a 'Christmas tree effect', whereby there was one light at the top and many lights beneath it. These lights were on an object hovering in the sky, just to the right of the path that leads over the canal.

They watched it for approximately five to ten minutes. Steven had the presence of mind to reach for his tape recorder, and recorded what he was seeing, which was verified by the two other people in the car. Towards the end of this sighting they watched as a white and then a red light dropped from underneath the object. The lights headed off in opposite directions – one to the north, one to the south –

then up into the sky, turning full circle around the object, then returning into it from opposite directions. Then, as they watched, the whole thing disappeared.

This was verified at the end of the entire surveillance operation when all the information gathered was studied. Other watchers at Knap Hill, despite not having seen the Christmas tree effect, did witness the white and the red lights at the same time that Steven Greer and the other occupants of the car reported it.

The very next day, on returning from Germany, I immediately went out to the watch with James and Gary, at around 5.30pm. At that point in time I hadn't spoken to my daughter or anyone else that knew what had taken place the previous night.

When I arrived at the top of Woodborough Hill I began looking through my binoculars at the fields below, and noticed a new circle. I pointed it out to Gary and James who quickly ran back down the hill towards their car. I then followed their movements through my binoculars, and they were soon heading along the path towards the canal.

They stopped just about level with the formation. I saw them both leave their car and walk towards it. When they arrived at the circle they did not enter. Then one of them stayed at the edge of the circle, while the other ran back to the car and left. In the meantime I slowly made my way down to the circle to find out what was happening. Just after I arrived, James arrived back with two guys.

They had two pieces of equipment about the size of two mobile phones. One was switched on and they slowly moved it into the circle by hand just above the ground. This was a magnetometer. The reading was much higher in the circle than outside. They then used the other piece of equipment, which could determine if there were any radioisotopes within the area of the circle. They discovered radioisotopes with a half-life that enabled them to determine that the circle had arrived 18 hours earlier.

When I finally got the chance to talk to my daughter and Steven Greer, it was discovered that the place where he'd seen the lights in the sky was exactly above the position that the crop circle had formed around 18 hours prior to our testing.

Out of all the circles I had been in at that point in time; this circle had such a delicate look about it. It spiralled from the middle, and slowly turned, until at the edge of the circle it was almost upright and touching the standing corn but just 3 inches lower. It also bounced gently in the breeze. Had anything or anybody walked in that circle you would have noticed the damage purely because each individual wheat stem was touching the other next to it.

On the last two days of that watch I heard some interesting stories from different people on the hill, and one in particular had me very concerned. It was brought to my attention that mutilations of farm animals had begun to occur around the world. Green lights had also been seen above the fields where these had taken place.

It was the first time that I had heard anything sinister between UFOs and life on Earth. I enquired more. Different parts of the animals were removed with very high precision. It transpired that surgeons couldn't operate so precisely, and not one ounce of blood was found in or around the area of the mutilated carcasses.

Apparently this had happened as close as two or three miles from where we were standing. I suddenly had a thought, Was it a wise decision for us all to be there, flashing our lights at possible murderers and letting them know exactly where we were? Or should we just beware of green lights in the skies. I had another thought! Maybe we're not dealing with just one E.T. race from one solar system. We could be dealing with several, and not of the same mind. I calmed myself by thinking that they must have a reason for doing this, and that it was no worse than what we humans do to animals ourselves!

It was on this watch that I first met a man called Michael Hessemann. He is a German who had come to England to film whatever he could to do with crop circles and UFOs. He'd heard that I had filmed a UFO, and asked if he could see the footage. So I arranged a night for him to come to my home. After he had seen the UFO film he asked me if he could possibly gain a copy of it. I gave him a copy purely because he told me that he wanted the message of whatever was happening around the fields put out into the public domain. He wanted everybody to know what was going on, and I agree with this.

Since then several other companies have enquired about my film and I have let each one of them have a copy. Why keep it a secret? It was the evening that I met Michael Hesseman that he informed me of a UFO conference that he was promoting in Dusseldorf in October. He asked me if I would like to attend. I may not have jumped at the chance if

I had known exactly what he had in mind. But that's another story for later.

Meanwhile The Troggs had a few small tours that involved Holland, Belgium, France and Germany. It was while we were in Germany that I found it impossible to keep quiet about what was happening in and around the fields of southern England. I began chatting to members of other bands, and I learned that as soon as you let other people know you're interested in UFO phenomena, they start to tell you stories of strange experiences that they have had. You may already be building up a picture of all the bands sitting in one dressing room and overhearing each other's stories. It wasn't like that. I received this information over several weeks and months.

The first story is from our own bass player, Peter Lucas. It happened to Peter several years ago, but he still remembers the night vividly. Peter was in his local village pub, which is situated at the top of a hill and overlooks a valley. He was drinking with a friend, a metal worker who made wrought iron gates and fire baskets. This was the reason they were both in the pub. His friend was to meet a local landowner who wanted a fire basket made to fit a specific opening at his home.

The pub had closed, and they were standing outside by the farmer's Land Rover chatting over final details. Peter noticed a light in the sky over the valley some distance away, which was slowly heading their way. When it came closer, they all realised it was a craft, and that a shaft of light was coming from it, pointing towards the ground. They continued to watch this object as it travelled slowly closer and closer towards them. The shaft of light went out several times on its journey, then suddenly it was almost overhead. They noticed a triangular shaped craft and from this a beam of light shone down to the ground a few hundred yards from them.

By now, the farmer and Peter's friend were trying to crawl underneath the farmer's Land Rover, but Peter had a different reaction, and was climbing over the fence that separated him from the light and the object. It seemed that whatever was controlling the object realised that Peter was trying to get closer. The shaft of light was extinguished, and a small light that was left made a square-shaped pattern in the sky. Peter then said, 'It shot away, directly up and was the size of a star within seconds. Then it vanished.'

They each decided to write, in their own words, what they experienced that night, and keep it hidden. Peter put his in a book. When I inquired about it, Peter looked but it had gone. So he asked his friends for theirs and, like Peter's, theirs had also disappeared.

The next story came from Ray Dorset, the singer from Mungo Jerry. He and his wife were travelling back home across the Hogsback near Guildford, when his car headlights picked up between eight and ten small grey figures, about 4 feet in height, running across the road in front of them. As they disappeared into the hedge at the side of the road Ray stopped the car, leapt out and tried to follow them. They had seemed to vanish in the night, and Ray returned to his car. They couldn't believe what they'd seen. They couldn't understand what they'd seen. But they did see them.

The following story is very strange, and one I have since

heard many times. It comes from Clem Curtis, singer with the Foundations. It happened at his home. He and his wife had retired to bed, and he was cuddling up to her with his hands under his chin. They were both lying in the foetus position. After a while he noticed something was moving in the room, and tried to move his head to see what it was. It was then that he realised he was paralysed.

He could still move his eyes and tried desperately to see what was there. He saw lights moving around, and had a drilling sensation in his head. He could smell burning, and found that he could move the fingers that were underneath his chin, and began pushing his forefinger frantically into the back of his wife's neck trying to wake her up, but didn't succeed.

The next morning when they awoke he told his wife what he had experienced, and asked her why she hadn't woken up. She told him she was awake but couldn't move either. She knew that he was poking her neck trying to draw her attention. It was then that they found a bruise on the back of her neck where he had prodded her. They checked for any visible marks on him, but found nothing. If I'd known then what I know now, I would have suggested that he get a head X-Ray too; the reason for this will become clear later.

In 1992 The Troggs had the great privilege of working with Richard Niles, a producer of much acclaim in the record industry. We were recording a fun version of 'Wild Thing' with Oliver Reed and Alex Higgins for the Christmas market. This took two days to complete with the video as well, so it meant staying overnight at the studio.

It was in the evening while we were having a meal and

chatting over different events that the subject of crop formations came up. Richard listened with much interest as I filled him in about what was happening in and around the fields of southern England. I finished up by telling him that I was lucky enough to film a UFO at the watch at Woodborough Hill.

He then came up with a very interesting story. Although not directly related to crop formations, I felt that in some way it was related to the UFO phenomenon. It turned out that Richard's parents are great friends with Uri Geller, and Uri had spent many weekends at their home. Uri has had many close encounters with UFOs, and readily told them that he puts his strange abilities down to this fact. Richard told me that on these visits Uri seemed to be forever saying he was sorry when things would bend on the table in front of them for no apparent reason.

One day just after Uri had left, something strange happened in Richard's home. Richard's mother has a thing about collecting buttons of all different kinds. When she sees some that she likes, she buys them and places them in a drawer in her bedroom, in the U-shaped bungalow in which they live. One side of the U is made up of bedrooms and on the other side is the kitchen. She was mixing something in the kitchen when suddenly, and apparently from nowhere, a button dropped down beside her.

She recognised it as being one of three she had on a card in the bedroom. So she went to look for the card. She opened the drawer where the buttons were kept, and rummaged through all of them until she found the card with the buttons that matched the one in her hand. The cardboard that held the three buttons was still intact, but the centre button was missing. It was the one she was holding in her hand. How, she wondered, did it get off the card without breaking the cardboard? And how did it travel from one side of the house to the other?

Towards the middle of August, 1992, I decided to fly the Alton Barnes area once more that season, in the hope that I would find what we were then calling 'the biggie' – the end of season formation. Unfortunately my luck was out, and it happened a week after I'd flown the area. James and I decided to go up on Woodborough Hill just one more time that season. I chose 18 August, because the previous year there had been several sightings on that particular day all across the world. The night I had chosen was 18–19, but the 'biggie' had happened on the night of 17–18 August. So it happened on the 18th, but the wrong end of the day. Also, it occurred four miles from where we were, near to Silbury Hill.

Slightly deflated, I began looking forward to the UFO conference in Dusseldorf in October. Through the whole period of 1990, 91 and 92 I kept on asking myself the question, Why am I involved in this? I had no interest before 1990, so why was it that I was devoting so much of my time to these phenomena. It was as though something was guiding me towards the right people to speak to, the right books to read and the evidence that I should be collecting. Which will become more apparent later.

It was around this time that I was guarding a closely kept secret. We had been asked if we would play at Sting's wedding. Sting, I discovered, lives approximately 15 miles from my home, in the area where most of the crop formations were appearing. I asked myself, Does he know about the crop formations? Is this a planned meeting by (what I was then calling) the overseers – that I should make contact with Sting, and perhaps give him information that he didn't have? Or was it just a coincidence? I flipped a coin and decided I would hand him a copy of Colin's video, *Undeniable Evidence*.

Just before we were about to soundcheck on the day of the wedding, Sting walked in. In the course of conversation I asked him whether he was aware of the crop formations, and he informed me that there had been one on his land. I gave him the copy of *Undeniable Evidence* and asked him to let me know what he thought. A couple of weeks went by when I received a phone call from Sting, who invited my wife and I to his home for dinner one evening. I took with me a copy of all the UFO reports I had to that date. So after dinner we sat and watched the video.

After the film, Sting informed me that on a skiing trip to Switzerland, while he was in the mountains, he and a friend saw what looked like the top of the mountain lit up like a Christmas tree (where had I heard that expression used before?), but as they watched, the light sped away at a very high speed. Before we'd met I had an uncanny feeling that he may have had at least a close encounter of the first kind. Sting and his wife Trudi are very interested in the whole subject, and I sent them many videos and books that year. Sting is obviously a very busy man, but I do feel that some time in the future he will have a part to play in all this.

After an interview with Mike Reid for Capital Radio, Mike informed me that he also had a close encounter of the first kind, in a park in London. I was beginning to feel that the UFO phenomenon was more widely accepted than I'd first imagined. I was almost beginning to feel that I had some catching up to do.

CHAPTER 5

The Troggs were booked to do a show in Edinburgh the day before I had to leave for the Dusseldorf conference. It was in the week prior to that I realised I desperately needed a haircut. As Martin, my barber, trimmed my hair, we began chatting and he asked me what The Troggs were doing in the near future. So I told him we were going to play in Edinburgh then on to Dusseldorf. I was willing to let him believe that we were playing in Dusseldorf as well, rather than to go into too much detail. But his next question was 'Oh, where are you playing in Dusseldorf?' So I told him that I was going to the UFO conference.

As soon as I said this, he replied, 'Are you interested in UFOs?' I told him, 'I wasn't two years ago, but I am now.' As soon as he realised that I was into UFO phenomena, he immediately told me the most amazing story about him and his then girlfriend, which happened in 1975.

They had been to a party in Swindon and were returning home towards Andover along the A345. I knew the road well. It used to be an old Roman road and is very straight but has many small hills. It passes the Swindon golf course where the event took place. He told me he was travelling at about 55 mph, when suddenly all the lights on his car went out and the car stopped. There was no feeling of braking. The car had just stopped.

He tried several times to start the car, but nothing happened. It was dead. He opened the door and the interior light came on. He got out and closed the door behind him. Although he was standing on the road, he didn't feel that it was the road. He also noticed that it was very dark, in fact jet black. He couldn't see anything, no stars, no clouds, no lights in the distance. He walked to the front of the car and kicked the headlights like a young guy would, but of course nothing happened. So he walked around to the back of the car and kicked the rear lights, but again nothing happened. So he then walked back to the door and opened it to get in. Then he realised that the interior light did not shine on to the road.

By this time his girlfriend was getting very scared. She was holding her hands to her face and kept asking 'What's wrong, what's wrong?' Then the lights began to flash, and as they did so the bonnet started going up and down on its own. Then it closed, but made no noise. Then the boot did the same thing as the rear lights flashed, again making no noise as it closed. Then the two front doors opened and closed beside them, again silently. The two rear doors did exactly the same thing.

By this point, understandably, his girlfriend was hysterical. He was at a loss as to what else he could do. So in a last ditch attempt he got out of the car, walked around to the back, and kicked the lights again. Still hearing his girlfriend screaming he walked around to her door and opened it, to try to pacify her. She screamed even louder because she could not see him while he was outside the car, which frightened her even more. So he slammed her door, ran around to his door, and leapt in.

He looked ahead of him not knowing what to do, put his hands on the wheel, and instantaneously they were travelling along at 55 mph. As though nothing had happened. On reaching Marlborough he pulled into a filling station and asked the attendant for some brandy to try and calm his girlfriend down. He told me that although he was only 19 at the time, he remembers it as though it were yesterday.

This event happened just two miles from Barbury Castle, where one of the biggest events of 1991 took place. A configuration in the corn that will probably keep scientists guessing for the next 50 years.

However, at that time I was unaware of the quality and the quantity of geometrical and mathematical information that we were about to obtain from that configuration. It wasn't until my return from the UFO conference that I became aware of just how important that configuration would be.

By the time my plane touched down in Dusseldorf and I'd made my way to the hotel where I would be staying for the three days, the conference was already well under way. I arrived just in time to see them all breaking for lunch. So I looked around to see if I could see any familiar faces.

Several tables had been set up for people to sell their merchandise in the foyer at the front of the auditorium. So I looked around to see what the people had to sell. Naturally there were many books on UFOlogy, but what amazed me most was the number of books being sold on the fringe elements of it – books such as *The Psyche of Man, Mythology and Egyptology*. I then realised why it was natural to link these other avenues with it. Often these crop formations were occurring near old iron-age forts, Stonehenge or other historical sites.

I then caught sight of Busty Taylor at one of the tables. After chatting to him for a while, I realised how important it was for these people to be able to sell their bits and pieces; it enabled them to finance their ongoing research into these phenomena. These semi-professional people are our only link to the truth behind these phenomena. We won't get any information from the government, at least not until something happens that they can't hide.

The next person I bumped into was Michael Hesseman, who seemed genuinely delighted that I'd made the effort to come. He asked me if I would be prepared to go on stage and explain exactly what happened in the early hours of 24 July 1992, when I had filmed the UFO.

Just after I agreed to do this I realised that apart from telling an audience what song we were doing next, I'd never really spoken to an audience before. Believe me, it's different singing to an audience than it is talking to one. Anyway, I was about to find out. It wasn't long before people were drifting back into the auditorium and it was soon filled with approximately 500 people. All of them were waiting for more information, from lecturers that had travelled all across the world. America, England, Russia, Czechoslovakia and Japan were all represented, and I was soon to realise what a nightmare it was for the translators. In some cases there had to be a translation into three languages. It was very off-putting for some people who had to wait for each sentence to be translated three times. It was also very difficult to hold your concentration while this was being done. But I was very impressed with the Russian contingency. Marina Popovitch and Valerie Uverov were very exciting. Although Marina could only speak Russian, the warmth and excitement she put across to the people was astounding. She told two of the most amazing stories.

Marina Popovitch was a test pilot for jet fighters in the Russian airforce. She went on to become a cosmonaut, married an astronaut, and to this day still lives at Space-City in Russia. I was amazed at Marina's openness to the whole UFO subject and her lack of inhibition to speak freely on subjects that I would have thought were very delicate to the Russian government.

She opened up her lecture with a documented account, accompanied by film, of what happened to one of their jet fighter pilots who was being monitored from his base. Evidently they were testing a new computerised fighter plane, and we were shown the locking-on procedure of the computer to its target. Suddenly a UFO appeared on the same picture, just as the computer was locking on to the original target.

Then it was as though the computer had become confused, and decided that the original target was not the correct one. It started to move towards the new target, the UFO. It was within a few seconds of actually locking on to the UFO when the UFO disappeared from the screen. At that precise moment all electrical equipment on the aircraft failed, and it was only the pure skill of the pilot that enabled him to land the aircraft manually.

It was Marina's high-ranking position that afforded her a place in the control room on many of Russia's space flights. She told of an incident that happened in 1988. The Russians had planned to send two space probes to the planet Mars. Their mission was to film Phobos, one of Mars' moons. This being accomplished they would then proceed to a lower orbit, where they would film possible landing sites for future Russian missions. The Russians had named the probes Phobos 1 & 2, and the two were to leave within three days of one another.

Marina was in the control room for the final countdown, when suddenly over the PA system a metallic voice told them to abort the mission. The voice asked them not to send these two probes to Mars and said that if they insisted they would be stopped. Needless to say the countdown continued and both probes were launched within three days of one another.

Nine months or so later when the probes were nearing their destination, the TV camera on Phobos 1 was turned on. They began to receive the first pictures of Mars' moon Phobos, when suddenly the TV camera onboard the satellite went dead. No matter how much they tried, they could not regain contact with the probe, and apart from those few first pictures that's all they received from Phobos 1.

However, they still had Phobos 2, which would arrive in roughly the same position in three days. So as disappointied as that may have been, they weren't too worried. They still had another chance. Three days later the camera on Phobos 2 was turned on. Again it showed the moon in full frame. Then something white and cigar-shaped entered the bottom of the screen and moved into the picture in between the Russian spacecraft and Phobos. It was estimated to be about 15 miles long. They were able to determine this because the object cast a shadow on the surface of Mars. When it entered the frame fully, all contact with Phobos 2 was lost. (See picture section).

Marina went on to say that in Russia today the subject of UFOs is now out in the open and freely discussed at all levels. Ten years ago people would only make jokes about the subject but now the attitude to UFOs is very positive. Around 80 per cent of the Russian public think that there is extra-terrestrial intelligence, and that this intelligence is trying to make contact with us.

'Cosmonauts and pilots are more ready to share information about their UFO sightings than ever before,' said Marina. 'Unlike the rest of the world, the Russians are now more open about the whole UFO subject, and once a month they devoted a whole television programme to it. In the near future university courses will be available to study the subject; several Soviet generals have already stated: "There is no question as to what UFOs are, we know they are alien spacecraft."'

During her military career, Marina Popovitch was twice awarded her country's highest military order, Hero of the Soviet Union. She has now retired, and is one of Russia's leading UFO researchers. As Marina left the stage to tumultuous applause from the audience, I could not help thinking how lucky Russia was to have such a wonderful woman at the forefront of this amazing subject. She made one feel as though she was talking for the whole of the Russian people. This was not some croppy from the Barge Pub in the sleepy little Wiltshire village of Honey Street telling me this; it was a Russian cosmonaut with photographic evidence.

The next person to take the stage was a young Russian university professor called Valerie Uverov, and among many of the cases that he had investigated one in particular stayed in my mind. It was in connection with something that I was beginning to hear a great deal more about – abductions. The abductee in this case was able to give a full description of everything that had occurred that night.

On 2 November 1989, two professional Soviet truck drivers, Alex Kusanov and his friend Nikolei were driving their truck towards Moscow. They were hurrying home to finish the paperwork related to their business trip before the holidays. In the vicinity of a filling station, heaps of sand and gravel, the result of road repairs, blocked the way in front of them and Alex was diverted onto a dirt road.

On one of the bends the truck's headlights fell upon a huge structure standing off to the right. Alex thought it was some kind of construction equipment. There were many machines there because the road was under construction. However, as he drove closer he saw a huge object that in the headlights had a metallic sheen to it.

Alex said, 'When we got to within 80 or 90 feet of the object our motor stalled, and we rolled a few extra feet. The headlights that were connected to a back-up power source were still on, and my partner and I could not understand what had happened. The road at this point had a bend in it, and the trees on the right hand side of the road blocked the view of the object, but we understood that we were seeing something very unusual in front of us. We were afraid that something untoward might happen.'

Alex asked Nikolei to remain in the truck to observe the events, while he observed the object. He left the cab and moved closer to the object to examine it more closely. After he had passed the front of the truck he became aware that with each step that he took, there was an increased resistance from the air. 'My body seemed to melt and I found it more difficult to move. I knew that if I got any closer to the object I would not be able to move at all,' he said.

Alex turned towards the truck and tried to approach the object from a different direction, and found the same constant resistance from the air. He succeeded in getting to within 30 to 36 feet of the object. He stopped on the shoulder of the road and began to examine the object more closely. Very quickly he realised that this object was not of Earthly origin. Truly it was something very unusual.

In front of Alex stood a huge disc-shaped object, approximately 130 to 140 feet in diameter with a dome shaped top, on which no other structures were visible. Along the perimeter of the disc, dark holes were evident, which Alex first thought were portholes. Extending from the lower part of the object two structures were visible, which seemed to support the ship. The far edge of the disc seemed to be elevated and was resting on some birch trees, two of which were broken.

The object looked dark and uninhabited, and there was no trace of windows, doors or edges. Why was this object here, at night, in the middle of the forest? What was its purpose? Maybe something had gone wrong, and it needed assistance. All these questions floated through Alex's mind.

Just then a glimmering red dotted line appeared to be drawn in the air in front of him, at the distance of an outstretched arm. It went on to form a square-shaped transparent screen of about 150mm by 150mm with rounded corners. Several words appeared on the screen written in red. Alex could not remember the exact phrase, but the essence of the wording was a request for burning fire.

Alex continued, 'I realised that the screen was illuminated on the body of the object. I automatically looked back towards Nikolei who was still sitting in the truck. Once again I observed the screen, but this time it appeared to be standing in front of the truck. I attempted to look from one side to the other, but no matter where I turned my eyes the screen remained in front of me. The distance to the screen remained constant, and I reached out my hand to try and touch it.

My friend Nikolei, who was watching from the truck, later asked me why I moved my hands. Alex said, 'The screen stayed in front of my eyes for the duration of the contact, and the messages stayed on the screen just long enough to be understood.'

Only then was the last inscription replaced by a new one. Only when Alex understood what was being demanded of him did he carefully back away from the object, constantly looking back towards the truck. Still sensing the same resistance. He returned to the truck and tried to open the right hand door of the cab. Despite the combined efforts of both men they could not open the door for a considerable amount of time. Then suddenly the door opened quite easily.

Alex removed a box of matches from the truck cabin, together with some laboratory alcohol, which was used as an anti-freeze for the braking system. Again asking Nikolei not to leave the truck, Alex returned to the same place on the shoulder of the road. However, this time he was able to move more easily. He experienced none of the resistance he had encountered previously. He gathered some dry leaves into a pile, poured the alcohol onto them, and ignited them.

Upon lifting his head he observed a passage that had appeared on the object, which extended into the interior forming a corridor. At the far end of this corridor he could see a bluish glimmering light. At first he had the impression that a shadow was moving inside the corridor, but then he realised that something was moving in there and was coming towards the opening. When he finally realised what was occurring he started to step backwards, and fell into a ditch at the side of the road. He jumped back onto his feet and continued to observe what was happening. Whatever was approaching the opening was a dark mass, which reminded him of a bag or sack.

As the mass moved it bent and swayed from side to side. Its periphery was very indefinable. At that moment a shaft extended from the object, which bent as it descended to the ground. The mass slid down the shaft and increased in size as it moved towards the fire of burning leaves. Alex was paralysed by fear. The mass stood by the fire for a moment, and then began to return along the same path, taking with it the box of matches. It then disappeared into the corridor.

It was only at this point that Alex extracted himself from the ditch, moved back onto the road and looked back towards the truck. The truck headlights blinded him, but nevertheless he could see the frightened face of Nikolei, which was pressed tightly against the windscreen.

For a long time, Alex remained standing on the road and was unable to recover his senses. Realising he was witnessing an event that he may never see again, he decided to wait to see what would happen next. He had a sudden wish to observe the ship more closely, and immediately an invitation appeared on the screen, which had remained visible in front of him.

After a brief pause he decided to get closer to the object. The first thing that caught his attention was the round openings that were about 300mm in diameter, which he had taken to be portholes. Inside these openings, at a depth of about 370mm, a grid of intersecting, light-grey lines was visible.

Alex was able to examine one of the support legs that the object rested on. The leg consisted of two parts, which enabled the machine to sit squarely on four legs. While Alex was looking at the support legs, he rested his hand on the transparent shaft that the mass had used to get on and off the ship. It felt cold and metallic. He had a desire to look inside, but since the door was above his head he decided to grab hold of the tube and jump.

The instant he grabbed the tube he found himself standing just inside the opening. There was nothing there in the form of steps or elevator, and he didn't feel any external influence. Everything seemed to happen naturally, or by itself. He thought of the possibility of danger to himself. At that instant, he received a message on the screen. The message said he had nothing to be afraid of, and that he could enter.

Upon entering the corridor he looked at the walls and noticed the absence of doors. The corridor was slightly wider than the opening, the floor was flat and the walls and ceiling were warped and oval. He walked along the corridor towards the shimmering light. He felt that he was walking on a flat metallic floor. He got the feeling that the surrounding walls were a secret decorative covering and something was connected to them from the other side which could have been for structural purposes. There was clearly some strengthening device that touched them. He didn't want to touch the walls, so he was unable to say exactly what it was that strengthened them.

He proceeded along the corridor for about 20 to 25 feet. At the end of the corridor he entered a large hall with a diameter of about 60 feet. In the walls there were five other entrances, similar in appearance to the one through which he had just entered. The ceiling and the hall were domed and emitting a soft diffused blue light. Between the other entrances along the walls there were panels of flashing lights. Each panel appeared to consist of five to six vertical elements. To the left of the entrance through which Alex had entered, two of the walls had no panels. In place of the panels there were horizontal recesses dark in colour. He observed two dark grey forms that looked like bags, which at first were motionless, but then began to move towards him. The 'bags' were identical to the mass which he had seen near the fire.

Alex stopped and stood motionless by the entrance of the hall. As he looked around the walls, a question came to him, the answer to which appeared immediately on the screen, but he noticed that answers appeared in his mind before he was able to read them on the screen. Several answers were accompanied by demonstrations of the operation of those structures that interested him.

Alex asked the question, 'May I know the significance of the dark horizontal recesses in the wall to my left? He was informed that the recesses were three-dimensional information screens. On one of these he was shown the interior of a sister ship, with the same moving masses on board. They showed the ship in space and many stars. At the end of the demonstration they showed the host of the Soviet television programme, Vienna. During the demonstration, the two masses aboard their ship remained motionless.

On the other side of the ship was an oval control panel or desk about 5 feet long, on which there were many switches and lamps. All the lamps had a flat, square shape. Some of them were elevated above the control panel and others were flush with the top of the panel. On the upper surface of the lamps there were some symbols, in the form of geometric figures such as concentric circles, triangles, quadrilateral figures, lines. The blank switches on the panel looked like toggle switches. There were no measures or scales on the control panel itself.

Alex described a large straight divan, which stood next to the control panel, and a circular crack in the floor which surrounded the central part of the hall. The crack gave him reason to believe that the central part of the floor could rotate, which allowed the control panel to be positioned in front of any of the vertical panels, which were situated along the walls.

On the vertical panels Alex noticed the same kind of lamps that were on the control panels. Many of these lamps were flashing. The entire interior of the hall was light in colour, including the floor and Alex said, 'The ceiling showed a soft blue light.' Looking upward, he tried to locate the source of the light whilst simultaneously asking about the measure of light.

No answer to this question appeared on the screen but in response to two other questions he asked, 'Who are you? Where are you from?,' the dome in the hall started to deepen and, as in the Planetarium, a star map appeared on the ceiling. While Alex was trying to find a familiar star system, one of the stars began to pulsate and then descend slowly. All the stars in the black sky combined with the pulsating star suspended over Alex's head, as well as the flashing lamps on the control panels, emitted enough light for Alex to be able to see all the elements in the interior of the spacecraft.

A minute or so later the pulsating star slowly rose and the dome re-illuminated with the soft diffused blue light. Alex was unable to study and remember the star map shown to him in any detail. He asked where the pulsating star was located. They answered, This is in your galaxy. Alex asked question after question. The answers he received were heard in his head before he saw them on the screen. What kind of ship am I on now? What kind of propulsion system do you use to make it fly? In response he was told, 'This spacecraft is a Scout ship and uses the electro-magnetic fields to fly.' He was also told they are studying our planet, which they use as a springboard to the future.

He then saw three masses entering the hall, and then a fourth. He watched a conversation take place between them and understood that the time had come for him to leave. His next thought was to leave something for them, so he took off his watch and wanted to place it on the floor, but at the same time he was told that they had a complete knowledge of the Earth and needed nothing. For the first time during this visit, they asked him 'Why do you use a watch made in another country?' He could not think of a reply.

Taking a few steps from the hall he turned and walked along the corridor to the opening of the craft. As he approached the opening, he took hold of the tube with his right hand and immediately found himself standing on the ground. Not looking back, he walked over to the ditch and crossed over the road to the same place he had stood a few minutes before.

He turned and noticed the tube and the opening had

disappeared. In a few seconds the outer rim began to move in a clockwise direction. Within around 30 seconds, the craft had begun to move anti-clockwise, and around it a luminescence appeared. As the revolutions became faster the luminescence enveloped the spacecraft, and it became a ball of light. Alex noticed that all of this was happening in complete silence.

At that moment he noticed two more cars on the road with their headlights on. For a few seconds his attention was distracted from the spacecraft. It was the sound of the tree branches cracking that drew his attention back to the spacecraft. The ball of light suddenly shifted position and began to rise. When it was above them it began accelerating and disappeared towards the north-east.

At that point Alex's friend Nikolei got out of the truck and, together with the occupants of the other vehicles, came up to Alex and asked him many questions. Alex was impressed by his experience, but at the same time too moved to speak, and did not fully realise all that had taken place. His hands and legs were trembling and when he got into his truck, he was unable to press the accelerator or shift gears, and had to let his partner drive. Alex leaned back on the truck seat and looked at his watch, which he still had in his hand. From the moment the truck had stopped 20 minutes had passed and they still had a day and a half's drive to Moscow, their destination.

Valerie Uverov continued, 'As you can see this is a very interesting case. And a question for the scientists; how did they use the magnetic fields? For us one question was very interesting; why did they ask for an open fire? Later during his contact he asked this question, and they explained that their spacecraft came from Orion and when they were out of the chronic corridor they had problems with their energy system. That is why the spacecraft was lying on the trees.

'As you remember the ETs looked very strange. This was an energy cover for the body. It was an energy defence, because this was the way to solve ecological problems of the body. Understand that they were working in high-powered magnetic fields, which is very dangerous for the physical body. That's why they use this method. They cover themselves with energy as a defence, and only then can they fly. But the energy system on the spacecraft had broken down, and they needed some kind of energy to restart it, so they used this fire to start the generator of their energy supply. So now you can understand what was wrong with the craft. So they are not gods because they also get problems.'

It was at this time that Valerie Uverov told the audience he could converse with aliens. He openly told the audience that to be able to converse with alien beings he normally had to clear the front part of his mind. For him this wasn't always possible with the everyday humdrum information that one normally gets. He then went on to tell the audience about some information that he had received about pyramids.

According to his alien contact, pyramids were powerful antennae to the cosmos. Apart from expanding the mind, they could also be used for healing. Apparently his alien contacts had told him that there were not enough pyramids on the planet, and that there was not enough cosmic energy being

Top left: The very first crop formation I ever walked into.

Top right: Busty Taylor whom I first met at Alton Barnes, on my first visit to a crop circle in August 1990.

Middle and bottom: Some of the earliest discovered crop circles.

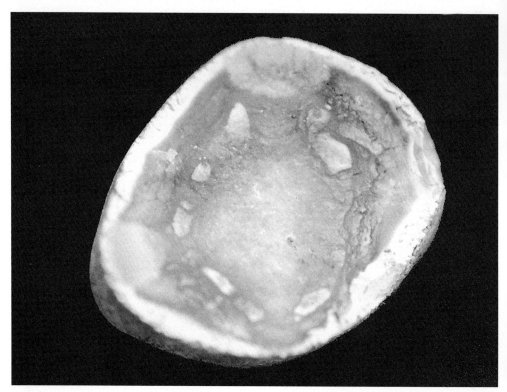

Top: Colin's flintstone with a replica of the inner circle of Stonehenge carved into it.
Bottom: I put my fear of flying aside to fly over all the new crop circles.

Top: When Busty tried to bend the rape plants on the edge of the crop formation at Sutton Scotney, they simply snapped.

Middle and Bottom: Bent rape plants.

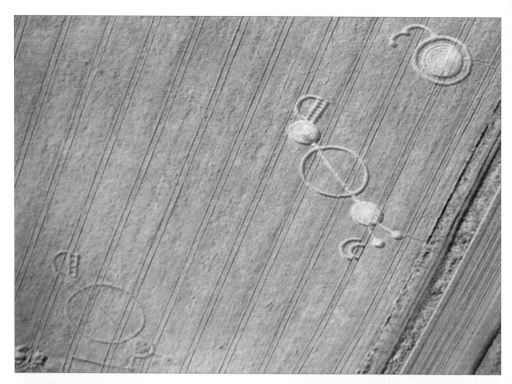

Top: Doug and Dave's insectogram: in the bottom left hand corner is the one they knew nothing about.

Bottom: Colin Andrews of CPR: co-author of *Circular Evidence* and world renowned expert on crop circles, who has gathered some of the most convincing evidence for alien activity.

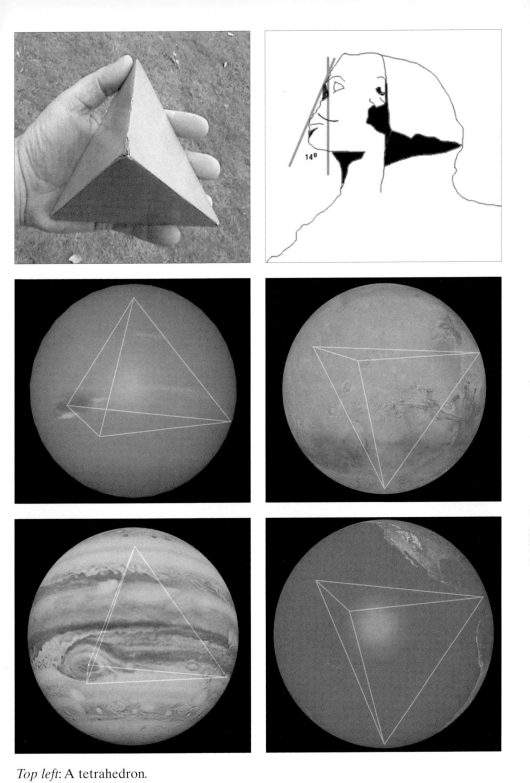

Top left: A tetrahedron.

Top right: The Sphinx: the chin protrudes 14% more than on an arabic face.

Centre and bottom: Tetrahedrons showing features at 19.5 degrees on Neptune, Mars, Jupiter and Earth.

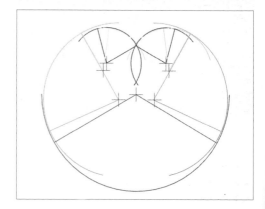

Top: The formation at Barbury Castle.

Middle: An aerial photograph of the Mandelbrot set. The pattern is laid down from one point...

Bottom right: ...however, this should be impossible – as you can see, the shape can only be drawn by using seven centres, marked here by the crosses.

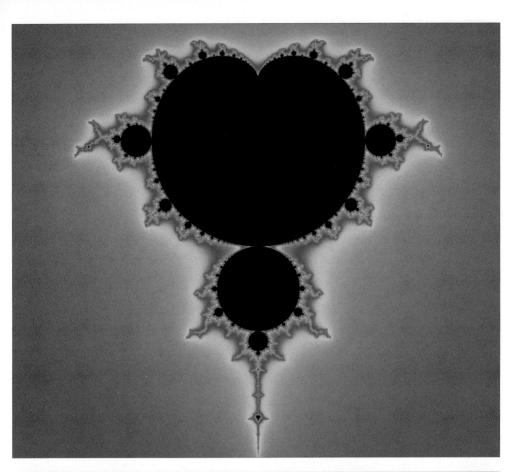

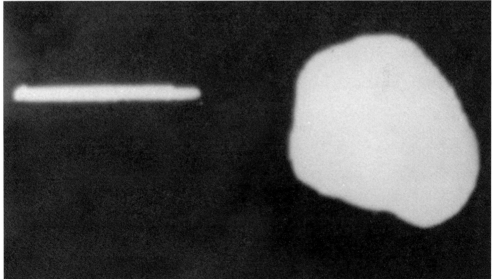

Top: The Mandlebrot Fractal.

Bottom: The only pictures received from the Phobos space probes before all contact was lost, showed a mysterious white cigar shaped object, estimated to be about fifteen miles long.

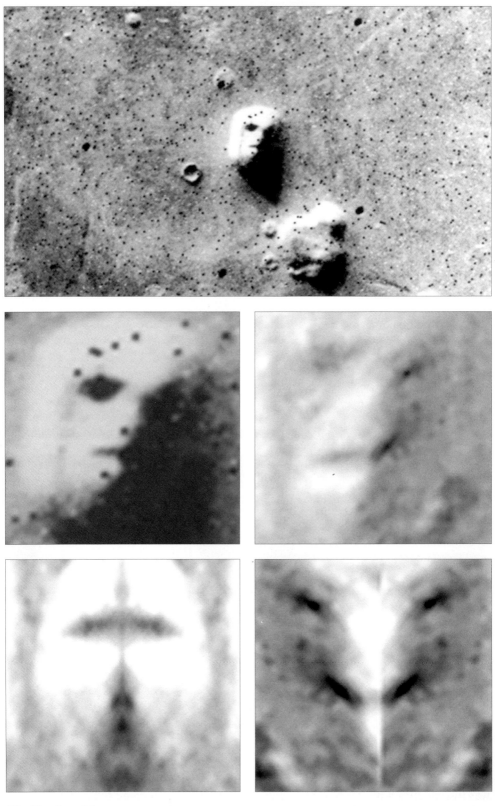

The 'face' on Mars

received. Valerie travelled to America, and spent three months there trying to persuade American architects to build more pyramidal shapes.

Knowing that he had failed in his attempt to achieve this he once again conversed with his alien contact. They told him that there was another way. If he could persuade individuals to build their own personal pyramids, if enough people built them then it was possible that it could put more cosmic energy back into the Earth.

He then invited those in the audience to participate in being measured for their own personal pyramid. In a room adjacent to the hall, 20 people came along to be measured, and I was one of them. A thought had crossed my mind that this may be some method of making money out of people's curiosity. I sat there wondering when the crunch would come, and I was amazed when it didn't. We in the West have been brought up with the assumption that people never do something for nothing, yet here was a man offering what he believed was an answer to some of the world's problems, free of charge. As I left the room I had a warm feeling that maybe there was still hope for the human race. Some people still care.

I thought it was about time I gave myself a break from all the heady information that I had been absorbing all morning, and headed off down the stairs in search of a quiet cup of coffee. Just then I noticed Colin Andrews and Busty Taylor heading towards the bar. Colin seemed excited about some information he had just received from America. After ordering a pot of coffee for three, Busty, Colin and I moved to a quiet part of the bar. With the help of my small tape recorder I was able to get the whole account on tape. This information was gathered at Atlanta, Georgia the first week in October 1992.

A computer expert had been asked to speak at this particular conference, because for the first time he was prepared to speak openly about a strange set of events that had happened on the outskirts of Atlanta.

Two years previously, in February 1990, he worked as a manager in a computer company and was commencing an ordinary day's work. He'd arrived slightly early, as a good manager should. There were a few other members of office staff in the building. He had just poured himself a glass of coke with lots of ice, and returned to his desk. He was about to drink the coke when he noticed that the ice was gone.

This was followed by a state of confusion, where other members of staff were coming out of their offices and looking at their watches. After a while they became conscious of the fact that the electricity had failed, including the back-up system. The computers had also failed, as well as their back-up systems and two hours of time had disappeared.

The company was working for the American government on computer analytical processes. Some of these processes are used in space technology and all their work is submitted to the government. This building is EMP protected, which means that it is protected against the electro-magnetic pulses which could be caused by a nuclear airburst. The premises were also lead-shielded for additional protection. Even with all of this protection, all systems within the building were hit.

The manager recalled, as did many of the others, being

lifted out through the roof by one of five UFOs that were hovering above the factory. He remembers looking down onto the factory roof while being teleported into one of the craft. While this was occurring, other employees were arriving at the car park to one side of the factory.

Because of the nature of the work carried out at this establishment, there is a whole network of security cameras, both inside and outside the building. These were not affected by the power failure, and all of the following events were recorded on video, which I was privileged enough to see months after the event.

All the personnel that were arriving sat in their cars for two hours and seemed oblivious to what was happening. The cameras picked up several small humanoid beings with large black eyes moving freely around the premises. After these events it was discovered that the incoming supply cable to this department had been cut in an absolutely precise line from the insulated sheets right through the conductors. A surgical type job had been performed. It was definitely not consistent with an electrical fault.

The manager and those colleagues that were abducted and taken aboard the craft. Each have an IQ of over a hundred. I almost anticipated what Colin was going to say. It appears that the entire work force at the factory was then shrouded by a veil of secrecy, with the threat of losing their jobs or worse. The manager has since left the company and is now practising as a computer consultant. He feels that the public has a right to know what happened that day.

It was then that Colin told me of a set of events, which, if they came to fruition, would be beneficial to all future UFO investigations. At the beginning of October 1992, and at very short notice, he was asked to attend a meeting at the UN, to press the General Secretary into implementing clause G33426 at the next general assembly. Clause G33426 is a policy agreement, which has been there in statute, waiting in the wings since December 1978. Grenada, which had many UFO sightings at the time, was also pressing for the clause to be brought forward.

Clause G33426 says this: that there will be an agency formed within the UN to disseminate, monitor and respond to research into Unidentified Flying Objects and associated phenomena. That is the precise wording. Which means, for the first time, we all have a platform, and it's coming from the place it ought to – the United Nations.

There was also a link between the SETI (Search for Extra-Terrestrial Intelligence) project and the UN meeting, because on 12 October 1992, they switched on one of the biggest telescopes in the world. What they were doing was monitoring thousands of channels simultaneously. In the first ten seconds they monitored more channels than they had ever done on Earth. They were monitoring across almost the entire radio spectrum, from the bottom end right up to the top.

Because their old equipment received several signals of the kind they anticipated came from extra-terrestrial sources, they are now looking to the UN for a world response. In other words, there has to be a global consensus in some form, because SETI are the chair leaders. They have the equipment to search out and identify anything that comes from space, but they need the help of all governments. Will they get it I wonder?

The three of us finished our coffees and wandered back to the auditorium, just in time to catch the tail end of Dr Jim Hurtak's speech about an experiment that he and a friend had performed in an ancient Mayan city in South America. Although I am not familiar with any of Dr Jim Hurtak's work I listened intently.

For many years Jim had researched into ancient Mayan culture, and had discovered that at certain times they worshipped a sound goddess. The ceremony would take place on the steps of a pyramidal structure. The ancient Mayans would chant her name on the steps of this pyramidal building in the City of Sound. Dr Hurtak was interested in ancient music and wanted to experiment by chanting the name of the Goddess of Sound on the steps of an ancient Mayan pyramid.

He asked the local Indian inhabitants what the name of the goddess was. Jim and his fellow researcher used that name to chant on the steps, but nothing happened. He then realised that the influence of the Spanish language had changed the name. It took him many months of investigative work trying to decipher old writings carved in the stone, before he was satisfied that he had discovered the original name. The experiment was then carried out again.

The day had been overcast, and there was an electrical storm brewing in the distance. The whole area around the pyramid was thick jungle. Night fell as Jim and his friend reached the bottom of the steps of the pyramid. Leaving his friend below, Jim proceeded to walk up the steps of the pyramid armed only with a tape recorder. He noticed that young government troops that had been on manoeuvres in the immediate vicinity during the day were now camped on the edge of the jungle. He could see their camp fires burning through the trees. There was a definite uneasiness about the night.

As he reached his destination, half way up the pyramid, a bolt of lightning seemed to say, 'You've arrived,' and thunder filled the night air. Jim sat down and turned on the tape recorder which he had placed beside him, and after a few minutes he and his friend began to chant the Indian goddess' name. At this point Jim turned on his tape recorder so everyone in the auditorium could hear what happened next.

I was lucky enough to be sat next to one of the public address system speakers, and was able to pick up the entire event on my own tape recorder. You could distinctly hear Jim and his friend's voices chanting for at least two or three minutes when suddenly a third voice, that of a woman, could be distinctly heard above their voices. It was not a harmonic; it was definitely a third voice. Occasionally you could hear the thunder rumbling overhead. Jim said he wasn't sure whether it was the thunder or the three voices that were actually making the stones tremor, but he could feel a vibration where he was sitting, all the time that they were chanting.

I must admit it was a very eerie sound. Jim didn't know whether it was coincidence or not, but when he had finished chanting, the troops' camp fires were out, and the troops themselves had left the area. Did the sound goddess join them on the steps that night? Some people believe that pyramids are antennae to the cosmos. Could that be a possibility? Where did that third voice come from?

When I arrived home from the conference, I quickly put the sound recording through my system and, allowing for a slight variance in tape speed which can alter pitch, I discovered they were chanting in the key of A, which is a pyramidal shape itself. It was then that I remembered Colin's diatonic tones that had formed all the white notes on a piano keyboard apart from the key of A.

This information, together with Valerie Uverov's and Jim Hurtak's, suddenly made me think that we may be about to discover some important information from the circle makers. It left me in no doubt that if not the A itself, the A shape would play an important part in the future. Eventually the A was discovered but not until many minds were locked into a search for it.

In fact a few weeks after the Dusseldorf conference, I discovered the real implication of what the A meant, of which more later.

The next person to take the stage was Commanding Sergeant Major Robert O'Dean. In the early 1960s, Mr Dean was with the organisation SHAPE (Supreme Headquarters of Allied Powers in Europe) NATO Intelligence Europe, and had access to a study conducted by SHAPE concerning UFOs and whether or not they posed a threat to national security. This is his story:

'I spent most of my adult life as a professional soldier, and spent 27 years on active duty in the United States Army. I was an infantry unit commander in Korea in 1951, and was involved in special operations in intelligence analysis in South East Asia. There were some "misspent years" as I like to call them, doing things I shouldn't have been doing.

'I must tell you very honestly that I began my UFO involvement as a sceptic. I was curious about the phenomenon and had a deep nagging suspicion that it was all real, but I had no proof. In 1963 I was assigned to the Supreme Headquarters of Allied Powers in Europe. I was privileged at that time to have cosmic top secret clearance. When I was assigned to SHAPE headquarters my first assignment was with the operations division.

'It was while I was assigned to SHAPE that I became aware of a study that was underway. It was a research program that had been established in 1961. I'll now give you some background into why the study and assessment was started.

'Throughout the 1960s there were incidences involving large fly-overs of enormous circular metallic objects travelling in formation and coming from the Soviet bloc area, over the Warsaw Pact countries. We estimated their size to be over 100 feet in diameter, and they flew very fast. They were very obviously under intelligent control.

'For a long time the Soviets thought that they belonged to the Americans, and the Americans were fearful that they belonged to the Soviets. Only later did they and we discover that they were from no place here on this planet. However, their appearance flying over Europe in formation at very high altitude and at very high speed almost caused the Soviets and the US to go to war three times. General Emnitzer, who was known as the Supreme Allied Commander of Europe and his deputy Commander, Air Marshall Sir Thomas Pike from the Royal Air Force decided that some study was necessary to determine what was happening.

'SHAPE headquarters had tried repeatedly to get information from London and Washington on what these objects were. London and Washington refused to send any information at all to the SHAPE headquarters. We found out later that the reason for this was a large French spy ring existing in Paris during the 1960s. This spy ring involved some top French ministers and a couple of French generals, and every bit of information that was available to SHAPE headquarters went directly to the KGB in Moscow.

'So Sir Thomas Pike decided that we had to determine for ourselves what was happening. The study was completed and published in 1964. It was titled "An Assessment". It later became known as "The Assessment". Its sub-title was "An Evaluation Of A Possible Military Threat To Allied Powers In Europe". When I had access to the study and had a chance to read it I was astounded at this in-depth study. I must tell you in all honesty that it changed my life.

'The study itself when completed was approximately 2 inches thick. There were supporting annexes. Documentation that was provided to support the study was at least 6 inches thick. The annexes were the most thorough studies I have ever seen. Several of them I will read to you. There was one annex on radar and electro-magnetic effects. There was another on optical and light analysis. There was an annex on photographing and holographic analysis. There was an annex on historical research and historical evidence. There was an annex on atmospheric physics. There was an annex on metallurgical and technical analysis. What impressed me the most were annexes on the physiological and psychological impacts of the evidence. There was an annex on sociological effects and implications, and one of the most important annexes was on theological implications and impact. Professors wrote most of that annex from a university in Germany. The reason that this document affected me so much was the amazing impact it had on the top generals assigned to SHAPE headquarters.

'We had at that time in Paris approximately 27 full generals assigned to the headquarters. These were brilliant military officers. The finest officers that each of their countries could provide. Now I ask you to consider for a moment the impact of a study of this kind on a professional military officer who has spent his entire life in his profession.

'I knew an American general by the name of Robert Lee. He was a 4-star American Air Force general. He had a long and distinguished career, and he was proud of his accomplishments. When he read the conclusions of the assessment, he was stunned. I shall read to you the main conclusions of the study that will hopefully explain to you why this document had such an impact on those military officers at that time.

'It included the entire NATO Military Air Alliance. There was an analysis and a study from Norway right through to Turkey. To give you an example of some of the material that was in the study, there was an incident involving a Danish farmer, just outside the city of Ulberg in Northern Denmark.

'A ten-metre UFO landed in his pasture. A door opened, a ramp came down, and two human beings looking just like you and I came down the ramp towards him, raised their hands, smiled and said in perfect Danish, "Come with us." He was a brave man and he was curious. So he went aboard for a ride. He was gone approximately one hour. When they brought him back they landed in the same place on his pasture.

'By that time his wife had called the local police, and because of what she had described to them, in turn they had called the local army detachment. When they brought him back, the police, the army and his wife were waiting for him. The farmer ran down the ramp excited, babbling, ranting and raving. He was waving his arms, smiling, excited to tell his wife what he had seen and where he had been. The army took him and his wife away for a week, and subjected them to what we in the military call a de-briefing.'

Robert then continued with another incident. 'Two days before Christmas in 1962, a young Italian Air Force sergeant was guarding a small airfield, just outside of Navora. It was very cold and at approximately 3 o'clock in the morning, a UFO ten metres in diameter landed on the runway. A door opened, a ramp came down, and two human beings came down the ramp and raised their hands and spoke to him in perfect Italian. They said "Let us take you for a ride", and beckoned him on board. "You have nothing to fear", they added.

'The young man was about 23 years old. Under questioning he admitted he was scared to death. He was very embarrassed when he admitted that when they came down the ramp and beckoned him, he had lost control of his bladder. He was so scared that he declined their offer. They returned to their machine and flew away.

'One additional incident from The Assessment before I read the conclusions. In the latter part of 1962 a Turkish Air Force plane with two pilots on board was vectored by its radar to a large object that had appeared on their radar screens. Ground radar control had also seen the large object and was also monitoring the aircraft.

'On screen the two objects came together. There was only one object left, the large object, and it flew away. They searched for two weeks looking for wreckage and bodies, but found nothing. This happened over land. If there had been a crash, there would have been something to find. The conclusion was that the large unidentified object had picked up the Turkish Air Force plane and had flown off with it.

'Now I will read to you the conclusions of the three-year assessment. I believe it appropriate at this time to tell you that I am divulging what I think are still highly classified secrets. I am violating my sworn oath to secrecy and silence. I must share this with you, because I believe this matter is so important that all people should share it.

'All the years that I was with the military I considered myself to be a loyal cold warrior. The cold war is over. I do not accept that there is any reason now to keep this information from the people of this planet. This information is what has changed my life.

'The planet Earth is and has been the subject of an

extensive, massive and very thorough detailed survey by several extra-terrestrial civilisations. These civilisations have demonstrated an extremely advanced technology, possibly hundreds or even thousands of years beyond ours. There also seems to be a process or a plan of some kind unfolding. Evidence has demonstrated some kind of program is under way. Evidence was collected by the study that some kind of program has been going on for a very long time, possibly hundreds of thousands of years.

'The final conclusion, which was the basis for this study, was that there did not appear to be a major military threat involved. If they were malevolent or hostile there was absolutely nothing we could do. They have been here for a very long time, and are intimately involved with our development and growth. I have concluded that there is evidence that there has been an intimate, inter-relationship between alien intelligence and the human race for several thousand years.

'When I retired from army intelligence in 1976, our military body and the government knew of at least four major extra-terrestrial civilisations. Associate friends of mine, who are still involved in government work, say that now they figure that there are 15 or 20 civilisations involved.

'One of the most exciting things to me is that one of those civilisations looks exactly like we do. This is one issue that caused the generals a great deal of concern. These visitors, these aliens, can put on a suit or a jacket and say, "Let's go out." You can sit next to them at a restaurant, or ride a trolley, or a train, or a plane and you would never know. You can imagine the impact that this kind of knowledge had on the professional generals at SHAPE headquarters.'

At this point Robert began showing slides to verify and classify some of the previous statements that he had made. It was whilst listening to Robert that I realised how much more information a man like him would have, tucked away in the dark corners of his mind, that probably even he had forgotten, and that we were probably just getting the highlights of 30 years of investigation into the UFO phenomenon.

I could not even conceive the kind of world that Robert must be living in if all that he was saying were untrue. The man would have to have a brilliant imagination to concoct a story such as he laid out that day. What would be the point? I know for a fact that speakers receive very little remuneration for what they do, so they don't do it for the money.

The three days that I spent at the Dusseldorf conference seemed to roll into one and like many of the speakers there I remembered the highlights. A Japanese astronomer was taking photographs of craters on the Moon and noticed that one crater in particular had changed shape. So he decided to concentrate on this one crater, and began taking photographs of it each night. As he showed the slides it looked for all the world as though someone was working in this crater.

One afternoon I missed lunch to eavesdrop on nine abductees, seven women and two men, speaking to a television crew. A Norwegian lady described an accident that she was involved in several years ago. Her car was a write-off, and – she believes – so was she. She remembered being beamed aboard a UFO, being delicately operated on, and then being put back at the scene of the accident. She is a doctor herself and knew the surgery that had been carried out.

Another professed that she had been abducted in the early hours of that very morning, and showed her scars and bruises to the cameras. And so it went on. Pieces of information day after day. Trying to absorb all that I was being told became a nightmare. Colin Andrews gave a magnificent lecture at this conference. So as not to take anything away from him, I must add that Colin's input flows throughout the pages of this book, and to have transcribed his lecture would have meant duplicating some of the information written earlier. Colin and Cynthia, his then future wife and myself sat at the back of the auditorium listening to the applause given by the audience to the final speaker.

It was around 9.30pm when Michael Hesseman asked all the speakers to return to the stage, where the audience was allowed to fire questions at each of the speakers. This lasted for approximately half an hour. I began placing my camera and tape recorder back into my briefcase and thinking of returning to the hotel, whilst listening to Michael Hesseman thanking all the speakers.

Although The Troggs have performed in Germany many times my German is still very sparse, but I knew enough to realise that I was being announced to go on stage. I couldn't help wondering what the hell for. I had already spoken to the audience about my film footage. Although in reality it was only a few metres, it seemed like 10 miles from the back of the auditorium to the stage.

The people had begun to applaud. It was pure luck that, above the noise, I heard Michael say that I was going to read my poem. If I hadn't heard, there could have been a terrible silence after the applause. There was no table handy so I threw my briefcase to the floor and opened it as quickly as I could to find the poem. A thought suddenly flashed through my mind. How were they going to translate this into German? Words that rhyme in English do not rhyme in German.

As it turned out there was no need to worry, because the applause at the end of the poem told me that they had all understood what I had said. Now, with hindsight, I feel highly honoured to have been allowed to end that conference with my poem.

CHAPTER 6

It would be tremendous if everybody could see an alien spacecraft, then all I have covered would become feasible to everyone. A sighting is the key to belief. There are many books and videos on these phenomena, but it is impossible for any one person to give you all the evidence. It has to be collected slowly and carefully. There are many intricate details to be gathered and logged in your mind, all of which are essential to piecing it together. Only the individual can do this.

To believe in these kinds of phenomena is very difficult in the beginning, and this is the sceptic's position. I was a sceptic. But three years' worth of information and a stroke of luck – with my first sighting – made me start to believe that something was being hidden from the public. On 26 June 1993, at 12.20 am, I became convinced. Around this time I had formed a liaison with a local TV cable company and would

host a five or ten minute slot on their programme about crop
formations and UFO sightings in the area.

Knowing I had seen and filmed a UFO the previous year,
they were keen to come along to a watch that I had arranged
with four other people, at Knap Hill near Alton Barnes. We all
arrived about 9.00pm and the camera and sound team went
about their job of setting up. There were many jibes from the
camera crew – who did not believe in UFOs – and for the first
part of the evening we were all laughing and joking. The time
passed fairly quickly.

However, it began to drizzle and the rain became harder as
the night wore on. As far as the camera crew was concerned
the night was over. They did not want to get their cameras wet
and decided to sit in their Range Rover for the duration of the
night. The other four people and myself stuck it out for quite
some time in the heavy drizzle. I told the TV crew that if
anything began to happen, I would flash my torch at them
because their vehicle was approximately 200 feet away from
our vantage point overlooking East Field, Woodborough,
Picked Hill, and on down towards Stonehenge.

At 12.20am a large silver elliptical craft, the size of a bright
half moon, sped across the valley west to east. The middle of the
elliptical craft was slightly darker than the rest. There was no
trail of the kind you would expect had it been a meteor. A
meteor was immediately ruled out anyway, because it was
travelling horizontally just below the cloud. Remember there
was heavy drizzle and very low cloud cover. We were
positioned high on a hill and the clouds were only about 150 to
200 feet above us. The craft was extremely low, and travelling as

114

fast as, or faster than, a jet fighter. There was no sound, and the craft was clipping the bottom of the cloud as it passed.

I quickly turned and flashed my torch at the TV crew, who were still in the Range Rover behind us. They responded immediately and got out of the vehicle. As I turned back to where I had seen the craft another, identical to the first, went speeding by. This was seen by the camera team but unfortunately not filmed.

At this point they set up their cameras and did a short interview with me for the programme. We spoke about what we had just witnessed, but because of the drizzle I could not persuade them to stay any longer, so they left. By around 1.10, the weather had changed from drizzle to full blown rain, and the five people who were left on the hill were also thinking of leaving. They were saying things like 'We'll give it 5 or 10 more minutes.' Little did we all know what was just about to happen! The strangest thing that any of us will probably ever see in our lives.

At precisely 1.20am we all witnessed a circle of light which came on in the southern region from our viewpoint. If you stretch an arm out fully in front of you, place your thumb on the horizon and open your forefinger to about two and a half inches, that would be the distance of the light above the horizon. We were later able to triangulate its position to be some nine miles away. It was turquoise in colour, and twice the size of a full moon seen from Earth.

Then even stranger, a white light came from this turquoise one and started expanding towards our position until it engulfed our hill and all the others in the vicinity. It was not until I was describing it to somebody about a year later that I realised what we had seen was not within any scientist's realm of experience or vocabulary.

We had witnessed 'slow light'. Impossible? No, that is exactly what we saw. It was as if you threw a stone in a pond and watched a large ripple coming towards you. Light travels at 186,000 miles per second. You do not see it travelling towards you! It's there or it's not. So the only way I can explain what we saw is by saying, 'It came towards us, so it had to have been travelling slowly.'

I'd like to hear any scientific response to this, but don't tell me it was our imagination, or that all five of us were on a trip of some description. That's the sceptic's way out of any problem. I now believe that if I, as an ordinary person, along with others can witness something such as this, then any government with access to the highest technology must have knowledge of much more.

So why aren't they informing us? We pay for the technology they use. Don't tell me they think we'd all panic and go crazy, because if that's the effect it has on humans then surely it must have the same effect on government officials. Hmmm, maybe the answer is as simple as that. After all governments don't act very rationally, do they?

For some reason, people on Earth have always had an affinity with Mars. When I was young, science fiction always maintained that there was life on Mars – purely because of the canals that some astronomers thought they saw through their telescopes. HG Wells's *War Of the Worlds* sent Americans into a panic when they transmitted his programme on the radio.

People actually left home and went up into the hills, trying to get away from the menacing Martian invasion.

That probably did more harm than good to the UFO cause. The government would have known for the first time how something portrayed as real – such as the radio show – would affect ordinary people. The problem was that they were portrayed as warring Martians, yet the vast majority of the UFOs we've seen and heard about since have seemed benign.

Now mankind has sent probes to explore the surface of Mars. What was once thought to be a network of manmade canals is now thought to be dried-up riverbeds. Since the Russians sent their two probes to Phobos they have recorded that 15-mile long cylindrical object floating close to Phobos. Also, scientists now believe that an asteroid hit Mars 500,000 years ago.

They tell us now that there was once life on Mars maybe whoever or whatever lived there before the asteroid struck may well have had the advanced technology to get the hell out of there. At the moment – to our Earthly knowledge – there is only one other planet suitable for life and that is Earth.

Could it be that a more advanced race looked around the galaxy for a planet that met their criteria and, over 500,000 years ago, found, on the outer arm of the galaxy, a suitable solar system? And on its fourth planet from the Sun (Mars) could they have created life as we know it?

Maybe 500,000 years ago those life forms were as evolved as we are now. Scientists say that 4-500,000 years ago Mars suffered complete annihilation from an asteroid that glanced across its surface. Rocks have recently been discovered in Antarctica that scientists say are from Mars – they have fossilised micro-organisms in them.

Perhaps their technology only had to be a little more advanced than ours is today, and the scientific community, the rich and the powerful, would have been able to leave Mars before the disaster. Perhaps there was only one other planet that they could inhabit, Earth. Could it be they arrived here in several spacecraft and landed safely in several countries? Their first job was to build a new civilisation, and with their technology (slightly more advanced than our own) they were able to achieve this fairly quickly.

So that generations would know the whole story at some time in the future, maybe the aliens buried their craft so that they could be used if annihilation threatened Earth as it had Mars. Maybe these craft and the megaliths that were built above them hold the knowledge of their species. It could be that when we have reached that point in our evolution, we shall be able to decipher the messages from the geometry of the megaliths and return once again to the stars.

I think that time is almost upon us. Our overseers are being seen daily around our planet, and they know that soon we will be joining them. But first it must not be a shock to any living soul. We must all know the truth. The experiment is over.

I received a telephone call from Busty Taylor who informed me that he had managed to buy a video of Richard C Hoagland's, *Extra Terrestrial Connection (Mars Mission)*. I recommend that anybody who hasn't seen it grabs a copy. Richard Hoagland was a NASA consultant, and co-creator of mankind's first inter-stellar message, currently leaving our solar system on board *Pioneer 10* and *11* spacecraft.

He was invited to give an address on 27 February 1992, at the Dag Hammarskjoeld Auditorium at the UN, and presented his findings to UN delegates, staff and invited guests. He maintains that, if verified, the evidence could radically alter our perceptions of the universe.

The images that he showed were taken 16 years before this presentation in 1976, by the unmanned *Viking* missions. There were four spacecraft – two orbiters and two landing craft – sent to Mars in search of life, but Richard, who by then had been working on the Mars mission project for nine years, never expected to find anything of the calibre that he was about to show.

Richard explained, 'We now have a set of data so extraordinary that what it demands, in the same venue as any decent science, is testing of the hypothesis. The problem is that there are some folks in NASA in charge of the next mission going back who seem less than overwhelmingly inclined to perform the simple test. They will not guarantee, as strange as it may seem, that taking pictures is on the Mars agenda. Well that, to my mind and the minds of my colleagues, is not good enough.'

I sensed more than a little frustration in Richard's words and with hindsight there was good cause, because in the latter part of 1993 when the Mars mission was nearing its photographic stage, NASA lost all contact with the craft. Or did they? It really infuriated Richard Hoagland and it showed in a later interview with the media.

At this stage I remembered what Marina Popovitch had said a year earlier about the Russian Mars missions in 1988, when they lost contact with Phobos 1 and 2. While I think about it, former astronaut and US Senator John Glenn was invited to play himself on the American comedy show, *Frasier*. On it, Senator Glenn turned to camera and said:

'Back in those glory days, I was very uncomfortable when they asked us to say things that I did not want to say and deny others. Some people asked, "You know, were you alone out there?" We never gave the real answer and yet we've seen things out there, strange things but we know what we saw out there and we couldn't really say anything. The bosses were really afraid of this, they were afraid of the *War Of The Worlds*-type stuff and panic in the streets, so we had to keep quiet and now we only see things in our nightmares or maybe in the movies and some of them are pretty close to being the truth.'

Why would a man like Senator John Glenn lay his whole life's work on the line if it were not true, TV show or no TV show?

Back to Richard Hoagland. He was showing some astonishing pictures of a supposed face on Mars. It sits there, in an area known as Cydonia, looking directly up towards the stars as if waiting to be seen by another cosmic intelligence. It is most definitely an artefact. (See picture section).

With the work of two imaging engineers, Vince Depetro and Greg Molinar, who originally discovered the image of the face in NASA's Goddard files, Richard and his colleagues have been able to perform extensive studies of the whole area around the face. The data that they have discovered and put forward (and, for the first time, out in the open) is so important that it demands scientific study, not only by American scientists but also by the whole scientific world.

I'm no mathematician but from the figures and calculations that Richard and his colleagues have achieved, I am left in no doubt that we are on the brink of one of the biggest discoveries in the history of mankind. Whilst looking in the area of the face they noticed to the south-west a pyramidal five-sided figure. And off to the south-east of the face they also noticed a mound, which has been called the Tholus. To the north of this is a dormant volcano and to the left of that a cliff. To the west of the face there are pyramidal shapes, which have been named 'The City'.

When they began drawing lines from each object to the other, a set of figures began to repeat themselves over and over. That set of figures was 19.5 degrees, and it was this that Richard used to decode the message of what he now calls 'the monuments of Mars'. To explain this a little better I shall use part of the transcript that Richard read out at his NASA briefing.

It says, 'The key to unlocking this multi-levelled interpretation which we've spent over seven years decoding now unmistakably centres on the geometric and geodetic properties of an inscribed tetrahedron. A tetrahedron is a four-sided four-cornered pyramid: the simplest regular platonic solid that can exist surrounded by a sphere (see picture section).

'If you place a tetrahedron in a sphere so that one corner sits on either the north or south polar axis of rotation, the other three corners of that tetrahedron will lie at either 19.5 degrees south or north latitude relative to the equator. Equally spaced at 120-degree intervals around the full 360 degrees, in 19.5 degrees latitude of that sphere.

'Some of the highly redundant geometric clues present at Cydonia now point us towards a connection between this fundamental inscribed tetrahedral geometry and basic planetary geophysics. The distance between one specific benchmark on the face, the so-called teardrop and another benchmark on the wedge shaped front of the five-sided Depetro and Molinar Pyramid nearby, turns out upon measurement to be exactly 1/360th of the diameter of Mars. Furthermore it straddles, precisely bisects, a 36 degree angle within the structure of the pyramid.'

Richard then proceeded to draw attention to the research of Errol Torin. He produced photographs from NASA's *Voyager II* mission of 1977, when the probe was sent to bring back as much information as possible about the outer planets in our solar system. The probe left our solar system in 1989 and is now in interstellar space.

The stills showed the huge swirling vorticular mass of energy which scientists call the storm, which sits in the southern hemisphere of Jupiter at exactly 19.5 degrees. It never moves. On Mars there is that huge dormant volcano, approximately 15 miles high and 180 miles wide, which sits in the Northern Hemisphere at exactly 19.5 degrees latitude. Most of the Sun spots occur at 19.5 degrees, and when you perform the same theoretical experiment with Earth, Hawaii, a volcanic island which has been active for probably 65 million years, lies at exactly 19.5 degrees. These are all energy upwellings from within the planets. (See picture section).

Richard continued, 'As the *Voyager* probe passed Neptune, one of the outermost planets in our solar system, it calculated, with the technology on board, that Neptune was giving out three times more energy that it could possibly be getting from the Sun. Add to this another swirling mass of energy sat at 19.5 degrees. It is now thought that if we could harness these physics that are working within the planets, it may be possible to create an anti-gravity machine. The possibilities are there.'

A Russian scientist called Vladimir Avinsky, in his Soviet *Life* magazine article in August 1984, called the face on Mars 'The Martian Sphinx'. This prompted further computer enhancement of the face. When they finally achieved the best enhancement they could, an experiment was performed using a mirror image of the left-hand side of the face.

To their amazement a humanoid face appeared. They then proceeded to do the same with the right hand side of the face, and in this instance a lion's head appeared. This discovery prompted them to take a more detailed look at the Sphinx in Egypt. However, when I recreated the same experiment myself (see picture section) I had to use a little too much imagination to create the same effect.

It was around this time that Richard and his colleagues discovered the work of a man who Richard describes as 'a rogue Egyptologist' called John West. John himself is a self-taught Egyptologist and had been working for many years on the Sphinx itself. He had noticed (and had tried to bring to the attention of other Egyptologists) that the erosion on the body of the Sphinx could only have been caused by rain. And the kind of rain needed to have caused that kind of erosion has not fallen in Egypt for between 15–20,000 years.

Until the present day, archaeologists and Egyptologists have led us to believe that the pyramids and the Sphinx were built by the Egyptians around 4,000–4,500 years ago. But now geologists, and in particular Robert Shock, have discovered that it is impossible to get the kind of weathering that is found on the Sphinx with only sand and wind. You must have rain. So we then have to ask the question, If the Egyptians didn't build the Sphinx, who did? Because we are led to believe that there was no other civilisation at that time with the capability.

This perhaps brings into play a name that is sometimes scoffed at by Egyptologists – 'Atlantis'. The name that has been handed down through time, myth and legend. Maybe there was an Atlantis. If you made that statement to an archaeologist he would immediately turn around and say, 'If you believe there is an Atlantis where is the evidence?'(And rightly so.)

Maybe the evidence is right under our noses. Maybe we should look at some of the questions that have to be answered before we can truly get to the bottom of what actually happened perhaps 10,000 or 11,000 years ago. What set of circumstances could conceivably arise that could wipe out a civilisation capable of building not only the Sphinx, but also the Pyramids?

The question of how the civilisation, be it Egyptian or Atlantian, that built the Pyramids was able to lift blocks of sandstone and granite weighing between 9 and 200 tonnes some 480 feet into the air has never been answered convincingly. How could this art, this knowledge of construction, be lost?

Today when we discover how to do something it is never lost to us again. We always retain that knowledge. If the human race learns anything today it is automatically taught to the rest of the species. It is written down, recorded and stored by every means at our disposal. Mankind will never forget how he got to the Moon. So why is it that no one can truly tell us how the Pyramids and the Sphinx were built? I cannot believe that brute force and ignorance built those monuments. So what could possibly have happened to make us forget? The only logical answer is a disaster.

Let us for a moment create a worst-case scenario. It is the year 2005; a plague has befallen the human race. There is no known cure. It affects everyone. People migrate from populated areas to avoid the plague, but to no avail. You are in your early twenties, for argument's sake you are male, you are a whizz-kid with computers. It enables you to afford a sailing ship and, as yet, you do not have the disease.

You stock the boat with as many provisions as you can, for a journey of an unknown duration. You invite three other friends, one male, two female, on board to sail with you. As you leave England the population has fallen from 60 million down to 2 million. The disease is still gathering momentum.

After a month at sea you pick up nothing on your satellite radio. You believe that the whole world has succumbed to this disease. You travel on, heading towards some desolate uninhabited island, perhaps in the Pacific. After six months at sea you are nearing the island where you are sure you will be safe, but then there is a terrible storm. You get smashed against the rocks.

Everyone aboard the boat survives but the boat is totally destroyed. All you possess are the clothes that you stand in. But you are safe, safe from the disease. Food is plentiful on this island and you survive. To your knowledge you and your friends are the only people left on the planet. As the last surviving human beings, all that came before will become just a memory.

Your instincts allow you to build shelters, to trap and snare wild animals for food and to gather fruits. But you don't have the help of such things as metal. Your life becomes basic and preoccupied with gathering food. In order to know the seasons you create some kind of calendar, some kind of timepiece. Perhaps you build a sundial.

You begin to flourish on your island. The women bear children. They have to be taught. But taught what? In the early stages, children would be taught how to gather the food and how to snare animals. At what stage, if any, would you begin to tell them that you came from a civilisation that could fly, and flew to the Moon? And how could you get it across to them that human beings built huge cities – some of the buildings being a quarter of a mile high? That there were billions of people on the planet? It would mean nothing to a small child that only knew its immediate surroundings. The whole idea of civilisation at that stage would be meaningless, and is then lost in time.

Maybe some of the stories about mankind would be told

around camp fires on your island, with children listening in amazement. How many generations of children would it take before the stories became myths and legends? Many of the ancient tribes that have roamed our planet for thousands of years, and that are still here today, have stories and legends and teachings from thousands of years ago which modern man writes off as myth. Is there any truth in these myths and legends? Well there seems to be something that happened 10,000 or 11,000 years ago, and it is written into all of the tribes' legends. With a little investigation it may become possible to extract the truth from some of these old myths.

The Hopi Indians of America speak of a great flood that destroyed their cities and houses and that sky people came and helped them rebuild. They also told them that one day they would return. The native South Americans speak of the Virracocha. This was a great civilising race that came from the east and taught them mathematics and astronomy. These Virracocha are described as being white with white hair and beards. Then there is the Dogon tribe of South Africa.

Like many African tribes, the Dogon people of the republic of Mali have a shadowed past. They settled on the Bandiagara Plateau, where they now live, some time between the 13th and 16th centuries. Bandiagara is about 300 miles south of Timbuktu, and for most of the year it is a dry and desolate place.

Although most anthropologists would class them as 'primitive', the people who make up the Dogon tribe would certainly not agree with this epithet. Indifferent though they are to western technology, their philosophy and religion are both rich and complex. Outsiders who have lived with them, and learned to accept the simplicity of their lives, speak of them as a happy, contented and fulfilled people whose attitude towards the essential values of life dates back millennia.

However, the Dogon tribe makes one spectacular claim. They believe, with absolute certainty, that they were originally taught and 'civilised' by creatures from outer space: specifically, from the star system Sirius, 8.7 light years from Earth. They back up this claim with an astonishingly accurate account of this star system. Notably, they know that Sirius, the brightest star in the sky, has a companion star, invisible to the naked eye, which is small, dense and very heavy.

This perfectly accurate account was unknown to western astronomers until the middle of the 19th century. It was not discussed in detail until the 1920s and not photographed until 1970. This is because Sirius B, as the star is called, is overshadowed by its much brighter companion. Yet long before, the Dogon would make sand drawings portraying Sirius accompanied by another star. We owe most of this knowledge to two French anthropologists who, in 1931, decided to make the Dogon tribe the subject of an extended study.

Marcel Griaule and Germaine Dieterlen lived almost constantly with the Dogon for 21 years. In 1946 Griaule was invited by the Dogon to share their innermost secrets. He attended their rituals and ceremonies and learned the enormously complex symbolism that stemmed from their cultural beliefs. These mainly centred on the amphibious creatures that came from outer space, which they called

Nommo, to civilise the world. Griaule also noted a kind of astrology, at the heart of which was Sirius and the various stars and planets they believe to orbit around it. They say that its main companion star, which they call *po tolo*, is made of matter heavier than anything on Earth, and moves in a 50 year elliptical orbit. All of which is true. Griaule himself was so revered by the people of the Dogon that at his funeral in Mali in 1956, a quarter of a million tribesmen gathered to pay him homage.

Another fascinating account similar to the one about the Dogon comes from the South African Zulu tribe. The Zulu maintain that their race built the Sphinx, and when we take a look at the face of the Sphinx a little later this belief may prove to be not so far-fetched. They also maintain that their people originated on Mars.

You may regard the statement as nonsense. You might even add that, until the Europeans ventured deep into Africa, that most African tribes including the Zulus were only capable of building mud and straw huts. If at this point you bring my theory into play (where the only way a nation can forget its heritage is via a disaster) then you would have to look for that disaster to even begin to find out whether there was any truth in the legends.

Now if we go back 10,000 to 11,000 years you have a disaster of catastrophic proportions. The end of the ice age. Could it be that the Mediterranean filled up with ice-melt? Could it also be that before the end of the ice age the Mediterranean was a fresh water lake? We are told that it is the oldest sea. Let me run a scenario by you.

Just before the end of the last ice age the sea would have been approximately 400 feet lower than it is today, because the water would have been locked up in the ice. It could be that the Mediterranean even flowed out into the Atlantic, at the Straits of Gibraltar. The Atlantic would have been 100 feet lower than the Mediterranean, and may have produced an effect much like the Niagara falls, only on a much larger scale. So perhaps no boat or ship ever sailed out into the Atlantic from the Mediterranean before the disaster. Hence, maybe, the stories we hear of falling off the edge of the world from bygone years.

If the end of the ice age came suddenly, as it's believed it did, 400 feet of water was trying to find a new home. That's 400 feet of water all over the planet. In all ancient myths and legends they speak of a great flood, 10 or 11,000 years ago (strange to think that Noah built his ark around the same time). Try to imagine that kind of water suddenly being released from the Polar Regions. The chaos must have been mindblowing. It's not just the mythical Atlantian civilisation that would have been wiped out but probably all known civilisations of the time. Perhaps they were sent back to the Stone Age.

When humans in bygone days built their megaliths, they did not usually build them in valleys. They would build them where they could best be seen. However, most of their towns and cities were built in valleys, purely for their water supply. So lakes and rivers would be the best places to be near. Even today churches and the like find themselves mostly placed on hills.

The longest river then and now is the Nile and when the

civilisation that built the Sphinx and the Pyramids looked for a place to build them, with no hesitation they chose the plateau at Giza. If, at one stage, the Nile delta was 40 or 50 miles further out into where the Mediterranean is today, and 2-300 feet lower, I'm sure people would still have lived at its mouth and around the edge of the Mediterranean, as they do now.

Whoever those civilisations were, they would still have looked to the Giza plateau as the place best-suited for the megaliths we find there today. With the growing knowledge we are obtaining about the ancient Egyptians today, it will soon be proven that the Egyptians inherited the Pyramids and the Sphinx from another civilisation.

If you positioned Atlantis on an island at the end of the Nile (with the flooding of the Nile, and the Mediterranean rising by 200 or 300 feet), it might have appeared from the mainland as though the island was sinking beneath the waves. After the great flood the Mediterranean would never have returned to its original level. Anyone living around the edge of the Mediterranean would have perished. Now why weren't they able to remember where Atlantis was? Because there were too few left alive after the great flood to pass on the full story and only the myth survived.

Many writers have placed Atlantis in the middle of the Atlantic. In his book *Fingerprints Of The Gods* (which has become a bestseller), author Graham Hancock has some staggering theories about Atlantis which are very feasible. He speculates that a great upheaval took place on Earth and that Antarctica was once Atlantis, though in a position much further north.

Then owing to a great polar shift and Earth crust

displacement, Atlantis (Antarctica) slipped south to where it is today. This is deduced from old maps showing the unfrozen coastline of Antarctica. He has pieced together the theory that Antarctica was in a much warmer climate. This was deduced from the fact that tropical vegetation was recently found buried in the ice. He has a good case and is quite possibly correct.

However, one has to question the dating of this Earth crust displacement. Was it a million years ago or 10-11,000 years ago? If that happened 10-11,000 years ago (as suggested by the author) and at the end of the last ice age, then one thing lets his theory down. If Antarctica was Atlantis but situated much further north, because of its size it would have been close to the coasts of South America and Africa.

If the Atlantians were a great civilisation (as we are led to believe in legend) surely trading would have taken place between the three continents, hence – perhaps – the link between the great pyramidal shapes we find in Egypt and South America. They would have taken their knowledge and technology with them when they travelled.

If the Atlantians were trading with their neighbours surely they would have traded the one great commodity that the Europeans had to offer – the horse! The horse is the one animal that has helped mankind progress as quickly as it has. Horses were prized. They could even help you to win wars – you couldn't win a war on a llama. However the Spanish were the first to introduce the horse to the Americas, and not the Atlantians (Antarcticans).

If the Atlantians didn't trade the horse then the reason must have been that the Americas were not accessible or were less accessible to them than Hancock's theory would suggest. This must surely put Atlantis back in or near the Mediterranean.

If we are to believe that any of the myths and legends are true, and many of them are beginning to have some validity, then in the case of Atlantis it is perhaps reasonable to assume that it would have been situated in the middle of civilisation at that time. If it was an island in the middle of the Atlantic, who would have been around to see it sink beneath the waves?

It couldn't have been the Alantians because they would have sunk with it. Sailors? Tidal waves created by the ice-melt would probably have made conditions impossible for sailors. It must have been people who survived on the mainland who witnessed the event.

The only people that would not have been in the cities were the farmers and goat herders, safely on the mountain slopes, who I'm sure would have not been able to build magnificent monuments. From then on, maybe it was just a story told around the campfire by those wandering few survivors, who headed south to high ground and on down through Africa, away from the Mediterranean and the great disaster they had witnessed. Could Atlantis be found at the mouth of the Nile, under what now must be hundreds of feet of silt? From boreholes taken in the Mediterranean, they know people lived where the shoreline used to be.

If, as the Zulu legend claims, their ancestors built the Sphinx, then the Zulus are descendants of the Atlantians. One other thing that supports the theory is the Zulu's language, which sounds very Arabic.

It probably took a few hundred years before very small

tribes wandered back into the area of the great disaster. One of those tribes must have looked up at the Sphinx and the Pyramids, and not knowing about the great civilisation that had existed there, thought that they were left by the Gods. Then that small civilisation flourished at the end of the Nile, and began to bury their Kings and Pharaohs in the places given to them by the Gods. The rest is history, given to us by Egyptologists.

What adds a little more weight to this idea is that the Ancient Egyptians tried to build pyramids that have been proven younger than the Pyramids on the Giza Plateau. And what did they build them with? Mud and straw.

John West and Dr Robert Shock have progressed amazingly quickly with their theory that the Egyptians couldn't have built the Sphinx. For their more recent work they invited Detective Sergeant Frank Domingo of the NYPD, a forensic expert, to take a look at the Sphinx. The Egyptians (Atlantians) were masters at carving. They would notice intricate details of the subject's face and would carve it accordingly. For example if one eye or ear was higher or lower than the other, every aspect would be carved in detail. In other words they were perfectionists.

We are led to believe by Egyptologists that the head of the Sphinx is that of King Chethren. So Frank Domingo's first task was to photograph the face of the statue of King Chethren, from the front and from the side, and then make comparisons with the Sphinx. He discovered that the chin on the Sphinx protrudes 14 per cent more than the carving of King Chethren (see picture section). In fact the face of the Sphinx was discovered not to be

Arabic at all, but the face of a black African.

Many aspects of our history have been hidden, sometimes out of ignorance or laziness, but mostly out of pure greed. I believe if the truth were to be known, in many cases we would have to re-write history itself. Of course there could be a more sinister reason. Napoleon's army was supposed to have used the Sphinx for target practice. That being the case, no wonder he lost the Napoleonic war, if they were only able to knock off the nose.

The Sphinx is a rather large target, so could there have been another reason for him only shooting off the nose? Could it not be that he and his entourage of catholic priests saw the nose of a black African, and the only way to hide that fact was to destroy it? Fortunately for us they failed miserably because as we have just discovered the jaw protrudes 14 per cent more than that of an Arabic face. So you see a possible reason for devious men at work, changing history. How could they let us know that the people they classed as slaves could have built something that they themselves could not?

Egyptologists throughout the 100 years or so have formed a clique, and will not allow anyone to undermine what they have presented to the world for fear of having to re-write history. And it's not just the Egyptologists that are the culprits. They are all at it, including scientists, physicists, historians, governments and the church. If you believe we have come a long way since the Middle Ages and these bodies of authority have changed, you couldn't be more wrong. Each one of them is joined at the hip to the other, and one will not release information without full agreement from the other.

When Galileo announced that the Earth travels around the Sun, the Roman Church had him tried for heresy and kept him under house arrest for ten years until his death. In fact it was not until 1992 that the church finally conceded the fact that the Earth was in solar orbit. The problem for the church was that they maintained the Earth was flat and at the centre of the universe. Heaven was above Earth and hell was below it. Unless heaven and hell were in motion too, they decided, the Earth could not be moving. And they were quite convinced that heaven and hell were static.

CHAPTER 7

When looking for the origins of mankind we would probably start at the Natural History Museum, because we would assume that anything of any significance that is found in or on the land would be there on display. Because of this we would assume that any one of us can gather the information discovered and add it to our existing knowledge of how mankind came into being or natural history has developed.

Not so. All that has been discovered is not on show. Items are hidden from us because they do not fit in with the thinking of the few archaeologists, geologists and scientists who are currently seen as leading the way. These scientists will, it seems, go to any lengths to stop new, challenging information, even when the proof is held in front of them.

In Germany it was the done thing to varnish old bones when palaeontologists brought them back from their field trips to the

Bonn museum. Unbeknown to them this ruined any chance of retrieving DNA from them. Then, for some reason, they changed to an organic varnish which enabled them to do so at a later date. In 1997, they took a sample of DNA from an ancient human thigh bone and discovered that in no way were humans related to an ape. If Darwin was wrong, as this suggests, why didn't this information reach the ears of the masses?

In 1880 California State Geologist JD Whitney was intrigued by a discovery made 300 feet under Table Mountain in South Africa. While digging for gold, miners unearthed a variety of stone tools such as pestles and mortars and ladles, in rock strata reported to be 55 million years old. Whitney made a thorough record of these finds and came to the conclusion that mankind could be much older than the then current evolutionary model suggested. Although Whitney well documented these bizarre findings, the general public and the scientific community know very little about it. Why is it that nobody knows?

In 1966 a team of American geologists were called to Mexico to date spear points that had been found at a geological dig. Among them was Virginia Steen-McIntyre, PhD. She and the others believed that it was a very ancient site, perhaps 20,000 years old. The method of dating they used was radiometric – which gives an actual date range – and they used two different methods to establish this. One was using uranium atoms and the other was using zircon crystals. When they finally confirmed the dates they discovered the spear points were actually 250,000 years old.

With hindsight she admits she would have been satisfied had they only been 20-25,000 years old, because people can accept a few thousand-year steps but not hundreds of thousands. Being young and naive at the time, all Virginia wanted was to get the facts of her discovery out to the world. It was not to be. She did not realise that it would ruin her whole career. Because she persisted in trying to get the truth out, all her future opportunities were closed and she has not been able to work in her chosen field since. The site was closed and further investigation was denied – for ever.

This is the automatic response of the scientific community if what is discovered does not agree with current thinking. People will not talk about it or report it, and that means that science does not progress as it might.

It is generally thought that the dinosaurs and mankind lived millions of years apart and, according to what is on public display we have no reason to think otherwise. However, when we add hidden archaeology into the equation, a whole new picture emerges.

Over a hundred million years ago the Paluxy River in Texas flowed across a muddy plain and many dinosaurs left their footprints embedded in the limestone forever. But the tracks of another creature have also been preserved on the banks of this river – the tracks of man. Archaeologist Carl Baugh has led the investigation into these footprints for 15 years or more. His reaction when he discovered the footprints was one of shock. He had heard about them some time before but remained sceptical until he began his work.

After he and his team removed layers of rock they discovered a series of footprints. Those of a dinosaur and, 18 and a half inches away from the dinosaur footprint, he revealed a dozen 16-inch human footprints. This was in the same rock strata. 'After you find a dozen footprints going left, right, left, right you have to interpret this as human kind.' Carl reasoned.

It has always been maintained that the footprints were a hoax to encourage tourists and visitors to the sight. Carl's answer to this was, 'Dinosaur and human footprints dived into the rock face, so we removed slab after slab of the rock until we came to the next stride of both creatures and sure enough there they were still together. I can only conclude this evidence is real.'

Most of the footprints have suffered from erosion, but Carl has one in perfect condition, which he removed after digging through the rock face. This footprint has now been analysed by Dr Dale Peterson, MD. After making several slices through the footprint, he checked to see if there were impressions beneath the footprint made by weight load. This appears as small contours in the limestone beneath pressure points like the heel and big toe and to his amazement there were, leaving him in no doubt of their authenticity.

In the same rock strata they also found the fossil of a human forefinger. It was put through a CAT scan which clearly showed the bone joints, muscle, ligament, and tissue. According to Dr Dale Peterson, MD it is genuine. The limestone layer that preserved these artefacts is reported to be 135 million years old, and as outstanding as that may be, artefacts have been found in much older rock strata than this. In Klerksdorp, South Africa, hundreds of metallic spheres were found by miners in pre-Cambrian strata over 2.8 billion years old, which are clearly manmade.

If the scientific world wants to disagree with these findings, it seems to me that they first need to check their dating system. Then our knowledge of natural history needs to be looked at again very closely. Because it would appear mankind has been on this planet with an intelligent brain on his shoulders for a very long time, at least 2.8 billion years. Personally at this stage of investigation I would suggest the dating system is wrong. They can't have it both ways, can they? Well, yes, they can if they keep hiding what disagrees with their way of thinking.

Just a few years ago a university professor, Eric Lathewaite, proved that a spinning object is lighter than a stationary one. He was asked to leave the university, because this goes completely against the Newtonian laws of physics. In other words, the rest of the scientific community would not only have had to rethink all they know, but actually start again. Now, because they do not want to do this, that particular science is in limbo. Which means we, the human race, cannot move forward at all on anything connected with gravity.

Gravity is an area of science we know little about. Now is there an alternative motive for this? Let us contemplate this for a moment. If we were able to find out how gravity worked, we might be able to use the findings to move from one part of the world to the other. Or from one world to another, using very little energy.

That being the case, there would be no use for fossil fuels. If we do not have to use fossil fuels we do not need oil. If that happened, it would automatically change our monetary system and would ruin the world economy (but would save our planet). You really don't have to think too hard about the direction we should choose.

Perhaps you can now see why they don't want anyone working on anything to do with anti-gravity. Anti-gravity or super-conductivity machines in any shape or form could quite easily be used for free energy. Hence the people that hold power would suddenly find themselves not so influential, not so powerful and, of course, this would not be allowed to happen. So the secrecy will go on. Unless of course someone defies those in power, and creates an anti-gravity machine in secret. That raises an interesting thought. Is it possible that some secret body of people, say the Majestic Twelve, have done just that?

The Majestic Twelve were first formed because of a supposed UFO crash at Roswell, New Mexico on 2 July 1947. President Truman formed them from the heads of the military, along with the CIA. They answer to no one.

Problems arise when you have ultra secret societies. They become so secretive that not even the government in power knows what happens within them. After all, a government is transient and can be out of power in only four years. That being the case a government finds itself in a no-win situation, if anything connected with the secret services goes wrong. People would blame the government for letting the secret society have too much say or power in the first place. But by then the government can get out of it by passing the buck on to the next government to follow them.

The MJ12, CIA, Club of Rome, The Illuminati, The Bilderburgs, The Mafia – no matter what they call themselves these secret societies only have to get one of their people in power every so often and they can bend civilisations to their will. No fuss, no bother. Simple isn't it? They tell us only what they want us to know and that is nowhere near enough.

George Bush Snr, who was President of the USA, was also head of the CIA before he became president. So don't think it can't happen. Could it also be that these secret societies have already got their hands on alien technology?

CHAPTER 8

Well, in 1947, something definitely crashed in the desert in New Mexico, and it was not from this world. In fact at least three alien craft crashed that year, but the events following them were confusing even to the experts investigating.

For the intricate details of events no one is better informed than Stanton Freidman. Any of his books will suffice. By now Roswell is a household name to most UFOlogists. However the implications of Roswell are staggering. Firstly, I would like to explain my involvement and beliefs in the Roswell film footage of the so-called alien autopsy.

It began just before Christmas 1993. Our manager at the time had just become aware of a re-released album of The Troggs, and was checking out who had released it. To do this, it seemed reasonable to contact the man who had the rights to do so the first time it was released ten years previously. This person was a Mr Ray Santilli. In the course of their telephone conversation, Ray asked if I would be interested to see a piece of film footage of an alien autopsy.

At first I thought our manager was joking, as he knew my interest in the whole subject. When I realised he was not, I asked for Ray's telephone number and rang him immediately. This was, as I say, just before Christmas. So I asked Ray to send me a copy, but because of the busy Christmas post it arrived just after. I played it over and over to visually gather as much information from it as I could.

However it was a very bad film and not clear at all, and appeared to have been filmed in either a tent or a Nissen hut. It was very difficult to see anything in detail. I needed much more proof to be convinced, as anybody seeing the footage would. I telephoned Ray and told him my views. He said, 'You haven't seen the best footage yet, and as soon as I have time I'll invite you up to see more,' and he began telling me what I would see.

At this time I had been invited to appear on the Anne and Nick show on BBC TV. I was asked to talk about crop circles and UFOs. So, with the promise that Ray had given me, plus the fact it was live television and nothing I said could be cut out, I phoned Ray and asked him if he minded me saying anything about the film. The phone went dead, and I had to say again, 'Ray?' Then Ray said 'Umm, okay.'

With hindsight I believe Ray stopped to think of the timing of his forthcoming campaign on the alien autopsy film footage, a campaign that at the time I knew nothing about. I believe like me he realised that it was national TV and live. Which means it was going out to 17 million viewers, but also, and this is the crux, it couldn't be edited out.

For my part I knew Ray must have more footage of better quality because I thought I knew him well enough to know he would not lie about something he could not back up. Clear in my own mind that at a future date I would be able to back up what I was saying, and knowing it would give the UFO world a kick up the ass, I went ahead on live TV and told them what I had seen in the tent footage.

Within eight hours, that news had gone right around the world and back to me. I had people from America, Canada, Germany, and Japan phoning me. The problem was that I had very little else to tell them. Everyone that rang me was told the same thing, 'As soon as I know more, you'll know more.' I had no intention of keeping things a secret.

Ray, of course, had other ideas. He didn't want things to happen too quickly because he was not ready to launch the video. But the cat was out of the bag, and even he was not ready for the onslaught that was to follow. With hindsight, if I had not given Ray's name on TV then I would have had the badgering that he had to endure.

Ray kept most other investigators including me on tenterhooks for another three months. Every time I went to his office the other film was not there, and always there was some very good excuse. I now believe even Ray was becoming frustrated by not being able to show what was on the film. I say it that way because I believe Ray had seen some of the finished footage at that time, but not all of it.

He began to tell people what he was reading on the canisters to keep them quiet until the film was safely on video. Many times in the course of conversation I told Ray to be careful, and to make more than one copy of the footage in case he was burgled. At first he thought that I was overreacting, and would just laugh it off. Then one day he received a phone call from a man who told him he worked for T42, an organisation made up, so he said, of the American and English secret services.

On the small amount of investigative work that I was able to carry out on the T42, I discovered it was either a Russian tank or a Tetley teapot! On one of the Tetley tea adverts on television I noticed T42 written on the side of the pot. Or it could simply be an abbreviation of Tea For Two. Take your pick. The trouble is it's so ridiculous we don't believe it, and that's how they get away with it.

Let's take it on face value. At that time Ray, through me, had told the world that he had obtained 1947 film footage of an alien autopsy, performed by American doctors attached to the American forces. He had himself stated to anyone who bothered to ask that the American President of the time, Harry Truman, was on some of the footage and that at a later date he would try to get someone to lip-read what the President was saying; the footage had no sound.

This was sure to alert any government connected to what had been said, but surely only if it was true. If a government did not believe that a UFO crashed at Roswell then surely they would have just laughed it off, and sued Ray for getting somebody to impersonate President Truman when it was broadcast on TV.

Or perhaps they tried another way. If they knew the film

could be real, then they would have probably sent in an investigator to see how authentic the footage appeared to be. If it did appear to be genuine, they would try to stop it before it came out. Either way they had to play it very carefully so no one would suspect. That is what I believe to have happened.

Just after I had warned Ray to be careful with the footage, both an office and a film studio that were involved in the duplication of the footage were burgled. Someone was trying to get hold of the master footage but, as luck would have it, they missed it each time. For the first time, Ray began to realise the importance of the footage.

Just after these burglaries, T42 contacted Ray by phone and asked if they could see the film. At first Ray said no. He was then pestered every day until he finally agreed to let them see it. At 2.30pm one afternoon the man from T42 showed up. According to Ray 'He watched the film very intensely.' When it was over he asked Ray if he could come back later that day with his superior, and Ray agreed.

I would like to have been a fly on the wall, to hear the conversation that took place between Mr T42 and his superior between 2.30 and 5.00pm. The first Mr T42, according to Ray, started off by taking the film very seriously. By the time he returned with his superior they were both beginning to run it down, saying, 'Of course you realise we have received dozens of these kinds of films this year alone, and if you tried to pass this off as real you'd probably get sued'.

If you analyse that statement, you quickly realise that there were two scared Tetley tea folk in Ray's office. 'They received dozens of them!' Even if the film had been a hoax, the work that went into it would have been so costly, and they had dozens of them? 'You'd probably get sued!' By whom? If the government sued, wouldn't that mean that it was real? I believe something more was said to Ray that afternoon by these two men, which changed Ray's approach to what he was about to do.

I believe Ray had personally seen all the footage at that time, and even shown all of it to the T42 guys, because soon after that meeting, when the President Truman footage came to be taken out of the canister it had become stuck together and impossible to play. Ray spoke about the Truman footage in too much detail for me to believe that he hadn't seen it. I believe he was threatened with his life that day, and took the Truman film out of play himself.

Let's face it, T42, the secret service or whoever they worked for could, and probably did, help to debunk the film footage as soon as it came out. But it would have been far more difficult to debunk if the world had seen President Truman speaking about aliens and standing by a crane that was lifting a flying saucer onto the back of a lorry.

UFOlogists investigating Roswell have discovered that the paperwork usually available from the archives for any year, is not available for 1947. It is as though 1947 did not exist. Just this in itself is amazing. What could anyone possibly want to hide? We may never know the truth about Roswell, but something crashed there in 1947, and it was not a balloon, as the airforce would have us believe.

Are they trying to tell us that the 509th Bomber Command – stationed at Roswell and responsible for clearing the wreckage, as well as for the bombings at Hiroshima and

Nagasaki – cannot tell the difference between a balloon, which is made from the same material as a condom, and an alien spacecraft, which is what they first said it was?

What has become clear, from all that we know as a result of the Roswell autopsy footage, is that it is from a different crash. This is something that Roswell investigators failed to realise in their blind panic. This panic was prompted by the idea that the Roswell Autopsy Footage may have been set up to undermine the confidence and integrity of the whole UFO fraternity.

Now the dust has settled, I believe it is the best thing that could have happened to the UFO business. Real or fake, it has definitely boosted people's awareness of the subject. You only have to turn on the radio or TV, or go to the movies to realise that. By now some people may be thinking, 'Well, if the aliens in the footage are not the ones from Roswell, then what crash were they from?' A set of incredible events took place in 1947. Many believe this was due to a new radar system that the Americans had set up at the Roswell Air Base that affected alien craft.

This is how the story sits at the moment. On 30 May 1947, a UFO crashed at Socorro, New Mexico, approximately 180 miles from Roswell. On 2 July 1947, another UFO crashed at Corona, approximately 70 miles from Roswell. And a third UFO crashed on 28 August at Four Corners, New Mexico. Before investigations began on the second crash, very little was known about the first. The second crash, Corona, became the most important, because there were around 300 witnesses. It was also released to the media before the military issued a denial (see picture section), and the story changed to a crashed weather balloon. The evidence for the first crash was taken to an airbase other than Roswell, so the people involved with the second crash knew nothing of the first, and vice versa.

The cameraman responsible for the Roswell autopsy footage couldn't have known about the other two crashes at Corona and Four Corners when he was asked to film the crash at Socorro (the first crash). In later years when people began talking about the Roswell crash, he believed they were talking about the crash he was involved with. This is why, when investigators began piecing the evidence together, certain details did not add up. They were talking about different events. No one has yet come up with any hard evidence that the Roswell autopsy footage that the cameraman took in 1947 is fake. In fact there is more evidence to the contrary. Fox TV offered $1million to anyone who could prove the footage was a hoax. To date no one has claimed the money.

If you accept, as I do, that extra-terrestrials are not only somehow responsible for life on Earth, but are also involved in an ongoing experiment with life on Earth and, further, that they even help us to evolve, it may be that this is supported by the alien autopsy film footage.

First, some background. It is a known fact that ancient civilisations used the 'twelve systems' for measurement – the same system that England used until decimalisation and America still measures in today – whereby 12 inches became a foot and 12 pence a shilling. The decimal system is relatively new.

You would think it might have been the other way around. We surely should have started learning to count in tens. After all, when a child learns to count, he or she puts up their hand

and with the finger of the other hand counts 1, 2, 3, 4, 5, and then to count the fingers on the other hand – usually pointing with his or her nose – says, 6, 7, 8, 9, 10. You can imagine cavemen sitting around their campfires doing the same thing. In other words, from the dawn of man, we should have counted in tens.

If you have seen the alien footage you will be aware that the aliens had six fingers on each hand, hence all their calculations would be in twelves. So who started us counting in twelves? It is not natural with ten fingers. Obviously had Hollywood made the alien in the autopsy footage it would have had three large fingers on each hand, one that glowed, and not six that almost went unnoticed.

Apart from the autopsy performed in the tent or the Nissen hut, I was one of the few privileged enough to see two other alien autopsies – one on 26 April 1994, in Ray's office (see picture section) and the other on 5 May at the London Museum. The first autopsy differed from the second in a number of ways. Firstly it was a different alien, secondly it was not damaged, and thirdly two different people performed the autopsies. A man carried out the first autopsy and a woman the second.

If the alien was just a mutant, as some researchers had suggested, then there must have been two mutants. The chances of that being the case are zillions and zillions to one according to doctors. If you believe the other rumour that was going around, that the alien was a dummy, but you accept my word that I was shown two different pieces of autopsy footage, then there were two dummies. Who made them? Hollywood effects specialists have said that whoever made them would have a job for life, but as yet no one has come forward. Surely this suggests that the film is genuine. Even Ray would have come forward to claim it was a hoax if he could have done, for the $1,000,000 dollars reward that Fox TV was offering.

One thing I have learnt in this UFO business is to go with new information when it is discovered, and not listen to the rubbish that soon follows. Most of this is misinformation. I believe Ray was offered the autopsy footage by the cameraman for the stated $100,000 dollars but, knowing Ray, he would have tried to get a better deal, hence the tent footage.

What better than to ask two fellows who worked for him from time to time, to try and come up with convincing footage of an alien being dissected to save him paying the $100,000? After seeing that tent rubbish he would have realised he had no alternative but to pay the cameraman what he wanted.

TV has only got an obligation to entertain. When the TV company first saw the footage they were as astounded as everyone else who saw it. Then they tried to gain as much footage as was necessary to make a programme on the subject. They would then have checked the ratings, and it would have been as a result of these that they made another programme and another and so on. When they felt they had exhausted the subject, this would be the time to put out one last programme debunking the whole thing and putting the story to bed . These programmes pay for the cost of the footage. Which, at perhaps £250 per second, is money that needs to be recouped. Their concern is certainly not with whether what is said or shown is genuine. As long they can get away with it they are the winners.

CHAPTER 9

If aliens are trying to find out how intelligent we are, and have been trying to communicate through geometrical formations in our fields, it could be that even the Roswell crashes were planned. Let me explain, having first added that this may seem far-fetched, but I feel compelled to put it forward anyway.

As I have said, the first crash happened at Socorro, the second at Corona and the third at Four Corners, New Mexico. Socorro translated from Spanish into English means 'Help'. The word Corona is used to describe the halo that appears around the Sun during a total eclipse. The Sun is a sphere. The only solid object in 3 dimensions with 'Four Corners' is a tetrahedron.

If the extra-terrestrial victims (sometimes called 'greys') were biological robots made and used by aliens for their menial tasks, then maybe it was felt that they were a small sacrifice to pay towards the higher goal of achieving communication with us. Maybe these events were trying to tell us about free energy sources. Or maybe extra-terrestrials were terrified by the threat of nuclear power.

Most people say, 'Why don't they just come down and talk?' Maybe they have to be a little more careful that that. When the Europeans first went to the Americas, they gave the indigenous people diseases they'd never dreamed of and almost wiped them out just through their ignorance. Remember that we are dealing with an intelligence that may be light-years ahead of ours, and may even be able to anticipate dire consequences in the event of a face to face meeting with us.

I believe the time is long overdue for the human race to harness free energy. Free energy is the most important thing if the human race is to survive. Each one of us has a duty to root out any conceivable way to achieve this aim. It is not going to be easy, because those in power do not want us to find it. It could mean the end of their reign.

Governments and the Church already know the existence of free energy and so do the oil companies. It may well be that free energy has been known about for thousands of years but hidden from us. Those who built the Sphinx, the Pyramids, the Mayan, Inca and Aztec temples knew of free energy.

When the Conquistadors and Catholic priests arrived in South America in 1532 they were led by General Pazzaro who could neither read nor write. This made it easy for the Catholic priests to goad him into annihilating the Inca population in the name of God and country. Whereas Pazzaro would not have realised the importance of Inca books and writings, the priests surely would.

Recently-published findings assert that when the Incas were asked, 'Did you build these temples?' they laughed and said, 'No, they were here long before us.' So when Catholic priests began destroying Inca books and writings they probably believed they had destroyed all knowledge of how the megaliths were built.

It may well be that the knowledge once used to build those giant megaliths remains, despite the church, so that we too can discover how they used free energy to build them. I believe the secret to the building of the temples lies in the shapes and measurements they left behind. Whoever built them.

I wonder how many of us that have become involved with crop circles and UFOs have a gut feeling that we are being used by some kind of outside agency for a specific purpose. Yet no one seems to know what it is. Could it be that we all have a purpose, and that we are being steered by this influence towards a goal that will become clear at a future time?

Perhaps everyone has a job to do and no matter how small that job is, it is as important as any other. Small bites of information will be added together until the whole picture becomes clear. I'm sure many of you have pieces of information you could add to the following, and hopefully sooner or later, we can collate them and establish their higher meaning.

Twelve years ago, not only was I a sceptic but I believed in mere coincidence. Sometimes I wish I were still a sceptic. A sceptic doesn't have to think, all he has to say is 'What a load of rubbish,' and that's it. He doesn't even have to justify disbelieving. On a TV show, I once heard a sceptic telling an astronaut what he thought the astronaut had seen out of the window of his capsule. Most sceptics disregard things which they have never seen or experienced. It's like asking a cod what it thinks of London.

The only way mankind can learn about something they've never seen or experienced for themselves is to listen to people that have. If we take a sceptic's view, if we've never been to Russia then it doesn't exist, regardless of how many photographs he sees of St Petersburg or Moscow, or how many people he speaks to who have actually been there.

As for coincidences, you know when something happens to you and you find yourself saying 'Wow, what a coincidence'? I now find myself saying, 'There must be a reason for this,' and I immediately begin searching for it. I have a gut feeling that one set of events that I experienced has something to do with free energy.

For some years I have been aware of numerology, but because I was sceptical I did not take an interest in it. That is, until someone awakened me to it by asking, 'Do you know your destiny number?' To which I answered no. Then by using my date of birth I was told that my destiny number was six.

The way this works is as follows:

- Write down all the numbers in your date of birth, (eg. 12/06/1941).
- Then add all the numbers contained within

this together until you get a number (in my case they equal 24).

- Then add the 2 and 4 together to give you a single figure.
- This is your destiny number. Mine is 6.

I began looking back through my life to see if there was any significance, any date that would be relevant to the six. And I found that six kept popping up. The date I had my tonsils out was the 15th: 1 and 5 = 6. When I married, the only day the church was free was the 24th: 2 and 4 is 6.

It seemed insignificant really, but my mind kept on seeing sixes. I even began to look at my room-key when booking into hotels, and frequently the numbers added up to six. I was, if nothing else, aware of six.

Suddenly what started as mind doodling began to take on significance. I now believe there was a reason that I was made aware of the six. In 1993, after watching Richard Hoagland's *Mars Mission* video, I began to add the numbers of the critical 19.5 degrees.

$$1 + 9 = 10.$$
$$10 + 5 = 15.$$
$$1 + 5 = 6.$$

When the tetrahedron is sat on one base the angle of the tetrahedron is 60 degrees, and you have three angles of 60 degrees. The fourth angle is the one it sits on, and the four sixes equal 24. Two and four is six. Three sixes turned up as a crop formation in a field at East Kennet twice, two years running. If I'm not mistaken the longitude where they were positioned was 1.5 degrees. Was someone trying to tell us something? According to Richard Hoagland, Silbury Hill is offset to Avebury's outer ring of stones by 19.5 degrees = 6. (See picture section).

Two old inner circles of stone are offset to north by 19.5 degrees. A crop formation turned up in the southern field opposite Silbury Hill in 1991, which had a right angled line, which in turn was offset to the two adjoining circles by 19.5 degrees. Now my search for the sixes began in earnest. I had to know if there was anything to it. The trouble is, life throws up distractions and things get put on the back-burner. Nevertheless sixes were always at the back of my mind, and it didn't take long before they came looming up again in the most pleasant of ways.

The area of southern England between Winchester, Warminster and Wantage where crop circles were turning up with some frequency is chalky. Chalk is well known for producing very clean water. In 1991 three and a half million gallons of water went missing overnight from a lake in Andover, my hometown.

It left six inches of water in the lake at a fish farm one mile to the south of Andover. In fact just enough water to keep the fish alive. A gentleman walking his dog late that night saw an orange orb of light hovering over the lake, which looked as though it was sucking the water out.

At the same time we had reports of three and a half million gallons of water disappearing from a rice paddy field in Japan. The only difference between the two phenomena was that the paddy field was monitored by sophisticated electronics. These two events (and remember Colin's stay at the farm of Mr and Mrs Jolly in Australia, where water from a dam went missing) jogged my memory about a documentary programme on TV some 15 years ago.

There had been two massive floods in Bangladesh within five or six months of one another. A German TV crew was out there making a documentary of the events and towards the end of the programme they had travelled up into the mountains and were interviewing the Mayor of the village. He was dressed in a western chequered shirt and a loincloth. Nevertheless he was the Mayor.

One of their questions to him was 'What do you put the floods down to?' The obvious answer to this would have been along the lines of, 'Well we cut down the trees for firewood, then the trees die and there's nothing to bind the earth to the rock. So when the monsoons come, the mud slides cause much damage and loss of life in the valleys'.

The Mayor's actual reply flabbergasted the interviewer, who nearly swallowed his microphone. He said 'I put it down to the silver crafts that come and hover over our paddy fields and suck up all the water – and it's got to stop!' The Andover missing water and the Japanese missing water prompted my memory of this.

Clearly, Winchester, Warminster and Wantage all begin with W, and geographically they form an equilateral triangle. (Sixes again, the angles of an equilateral triangle being 60 degrees.) I changed the Ws into numbers. W is the 23rd letter of the alphabet and we have three of them here.

23 + 23 +23 = 69.

6 + 9 = 15.

1 + 5 = 6.

At this time I was still struggling with coincidences. Was it all just chance? Then, as if to cement everything, and let me know that I was on the right lines, Wet Wet Wet covered a song that I had written 28 years previously. Of all the bands that could have recorded it, it had to be Wet Wet Wet.

Immediately I went to work on the sixes and the most amazing thing developed. Now because I had worked out the Winchester, Warminster and Wantage theory by commencing with the W's, that is how I began with Wet Wet Wet. I added the W's first then the E's which is the 5th letter of the alphabet then the T's the 20th.

A B C D E F G H I J K L M N O P Q R S T U V W X Y Z

1 2 3 4 5 6 7 8 9 10 11 12 13 14 15 16 17 18 19 20 21 22 23 24 25 26

WWW

23+23+23=69

6+9=15.

1+5=6.

EEE

5+5+5=15.

1+5=6.

TTT

20+20+20=60.

6+0=6.

The title of the song they had covered was 'Love Is All Around' which consists of 15 letters. $1 + 5 = 6$. I say again that of all the bands that could have recorded that song, it was as good as saying WATER, WATER, WATER. But it didn't stop there. 'Love Is All Around' entered the chart at number 4. Then in the second week went to number 2. $2 + 4 = 6$. It stayed at No 1 for a phenomenal 15 weeks. $1 + 5 = 6$.

The next piece of information is unusual if nothing else. It was in the chart for 23 weeks, and then dropped out. It had stayed in the chart so long it was almost Christmas. We believe people started buying it for each other for Christmas, because it went back into the charts for one more week. Making it a total of 24 weeks. $2 + 4 = 6$.

Top of the Pops phoned me and asked me if I would introduce Wet Wet Wet on their programme. I was on holiday at the time but agreed. When did they want me to introduce them? The sixth week that it was at number 1. From that point on I became more aware of other references to the magic six.

It seemed as though the three sixes would appear in the forefront, but you would have to look for the fourth six, in order to make those numbers add up. But it would be there, somewhere.

I received a video from someone in the post. The gentleman hosting the video was talking about Area 51, the Top Secret Air Force base in the Nevada desert in America where it is believed that scientists are back-engineering crashed UFOs. However, it is now possible to buy aerial reconnaissance photographs of the base from the Russians for $2,000. According to American officials Area 51 does not exist. The host also mentioned that the road leading to Area 51 was named Route 666. Here we go again. Three plain sixes, plus the 5 + 1 of area 51.

It had not escaped my attention that 666 was also the number of the beast. I became interested to find out what was said about it in the Bible, so I went out and bought my first Bible and read Revelations. It said, 'Anybody who has wisdom and intelligence can work out the name of the beast from 666'. It also says the name will be human.

Why, I thought, if Christianity wants us to steer clear of the beast, didn't they print the devil's name for all to see? Why hide it? Why was it left to only the wise and intelligent to work it out? I began to use wisdom, intelligence and numerology as a guide and proceeded to change 666 into letters. I looked at the alphabet and changed numbers for letters.

The first six is F. (The sixth letter of the alphabet.)
The second six is O. (The 15th letter of the alphabet: 1 + 5 = 6.)
The third six is X. (The 24th letter of the alphabet: 2 + 4 = 6.)

So we have FOX. But is fox a human name? Well yes it is, but it is also a beast. Sit well together don't they? My mind began racing. Fox TV is a huge American TV company that makes some of the better UFO programmes. *Independence Day*, the movie, was the biggest box office draw of 1996 made by Twentieth Century Fox. Remember the sixes. Fox equals 666. 'Independence Day' has 15 letters. 1 + 5 = 6. Not only this, but the TV programme with one of the highest ratings was *The X Files*, and David Duchovny who plays the main character is called Fox Mulder. Fox being the 666. 'Mulder' contains six letters, the hidden six. Could it have been without thinking that the writer of *The X Files* named him Fox Mulder? Remember the CIA agent that tracked down Colin. He was supposedly doing research on foxes.

Other things began springing to mind as soon as the word fox appeared. For instance, the jackal is similar to a fox and both are from the dog family. Wasn't it because of a jackal they found one of the tombs in Egypt? I started wondering why the Egyptian fox (Anubis) pops up as carvings and statues outside many Egyptian tombs. I was on a roll, so I let my imagination continue to take me along.

Dog spelt backwards is 'god'. To live we believe is good, but spelt backwards it is 'evil'. Lived spelt backwards is 'devil'. Not only did these words seemed to me to be very close, but there is a fine line between good and evil. Really important things are often subtle and finely-tuned.

The way we live should be in balance, but most of the time our technology sends it haywire. Mother Nature knows we have thinking minds (and probably wonders why we don't use them more often), and left to her own devices she leads us to the answer that will benefit all. With this in mind it seems likely that, as well as the pyramid-makers, Mother Nature is trying to give us clues that will lead us to free energy. Is it pure coincidence? Or is it something that comes from the ether, something that is drawn from our very being. Then something else came into my mind.

If the Church and the government have always known about free energy and 666 is somehow connected to free energy or gravity then perhaps it makes sense to assume that they would hide the evidence as long as possible. You see even a scientist with a religious background might have steered clear of anything related to 666, at least in the early years of science. The number of the beast (666) is so deeply rooted in our psyche, that it is not even possible to obtain a numberplate from the DVLA with the numbers 666 on it. They refuse to allocate them.

Everything mankind needs to know is already in front of him in nature. And when the time is right, technology catches up. Man saw birds fly before he could fly himself, but he knew flight was possible because the birds were doing it. Mankind must have sat and watched lightning for thousands of years, but look how long it took him to harness electricity. Mankind also sits and watches the planets going round in free space. When will he realise that the way the planets operate shows the way we will eventually conquer space. Earth has its own gravity, mankind has to reason out the workings of gravity, not avoid it as they have been.

The scientist mentioned previously, Professor Eric Lathewaite, who showed that a spinning object is lighter than a stationary one, used apparatus consisting of a heavy metal brass wheel on the end of an axle. In the experiment he tried to lift the wheel above shoulder height while keeping his arm straight, and found it impossible.

He then spun the wheel at high speed and found that he could lift the wheel easily over his head at arm's length. He then proceeded to do the same experiment, only this time during the experiment he weighed himself both when the wheel was stationary and when it was spinning. He discovered that he was 5 pounds lighter during the experiment with the spinning wheel.

This goes completely against Newtonian law. It would have meant that all the prior knowledge that Newton had laid down (which is the equivalent of the Bible to a scientist) was wrong. The Galileo scenario still happens today. Nothing has changed.

However, back to the sixes. Summer 1996 gave us a splendid formation in the shape of nature's spiral (now known as the Julia Set) in the field opposite Stonehenge. Also near Windmill Hill were three natural spirals, again nature's three sixes. I now believe that crop formations have several functions. One is to inform, one is to re-educate and another is to heal.

If humans weren't so preoccupied with making money, we would not have lost our ability to understand the meaning of life itself. We are being shown certain patterns that we should already know.

For aborigines, a simple circle written on a rock means 'water'. Hence, when they want to let others know how much water there is at the next well, they draw more circles around the first one. The more circles there are, the more water there is. (This makes sense; if you throw a stone into water it creates ripples, and the more ripples the greater the area of water covered.)

If an outside intelligence is trying to communicate through

geometry, it seems logical to assume that they would commence with simple forms which all intelligent life should understand, gradually making things more complex. Since those early circles, each year the formations have become more complex and have to be deciphered. One formation in particular which appeared south of Silbury Hill in 1994 was begging to be interpreted as 'the string of pearls', like the asteroid that hit Jupiter in 1995. It was named the Scorpion. (See picture section).

Could this have been a message to us that they knew about the asteroid before the event? Something else happened connected with the scorpion pattern. In May 1994, I was asked to do many press interviews, because of the success of 'Love Is All Around'. Each journalist wanted me to speak about my interest in crop formations, as well as my music. It was early in the season and only a few formations had appeared.

Each journalist wanted me to be photographed in or near crop formations. I did not want to have photographs taken in or near the same crop formation, so I was running out of new crop formations fast. On 21 May I was driving towards the car park at Silbury Hill, where I had planned to meet one of England's top journalists. The plan was to meet there and shoot off to a circle of my choice. All the way there I was racking my brains to think where I could take this journalist. As I passed a field, just before Silbury Hill on the left, there was a huge configuration. The Scorpion had arrived.

It was not there the previous day, and it had rained very heavily all night. I could not have wished for anything better. I could not wait to phone Colin, who by then was living in the

States with his wife Cynthia. As soon as I arrived home I phoned Colin and described what I had seen.

He then told me that ten minutes before I had phoned he'd had Tlakaelel, the Mexican Aztec Elder, visit his home. Colin told me that the reason for his visit was that he was in search of a particular pattern. He had evidently had a spiritual calling and was told to look for a pattern in 'The place of the last ceremonial dance'.

He described what pattern he was looking for, and although Colin showed him most of the patterns from his database he was unable to find the right one. It seemed to be a mixture of several. As you've probably guessed, the Scorpion was the one the Aztec elder was looking for. So is Silbury the place of 'The last ceremonial dance'? Not even Tlakaelel could say for sure.

Tlakaelel's first visit to England took place two years later in 1996. He could not wait to stand in the field of the scorpion (see picture section). When I met him, although he is a small man in stature I felt humble in his presence. He has almost 300 years of Aztec history and knowledge in his head. I'm sure one day soon mankind will need his help and that of other native Americans to get the human race back on the right path.

In July 1995 a crop formation turned up in a field of wheat within the Winchester/Warminster/Wantage triangle. An aerial photograph was taken and sent to America for analysis by two professors of mathematics, who worked on the photographs for several months. They concluded that the crop formation was a diagram of our solar system. It showed the four inner orbits of Mercury,

Venus, Earth and Mars. Worryingly, if the professors are correct, Earth is missing from its orbit. (See picture section)

The small circles you see around the outside of the planetary orbits are supposed to be the asteroid belt. Even stranger is the fact that one month after this crop formation appeared, two amateur astronomers called Hale and Bopp discovered a colossal comet (now called Hale-Bopp) heading towards Earth. Each time I enquired as to how close it would come to the Earth, the distance was halved.

The first time I asked it was 240 million miles away. Three months later it was 120 million miles. So in September 1996 I decided to phone the observatory at Jodrell Bank to get an answer from a professional body. The gentleman I spoke to gave me a then accurate figure of 80 million miles. If the first set of figures was correct, I hesitated to ask how close it would come when Hale-Bopp was at its closest position, on 23 March 1997. Thankfully, as we now know, Hale-Bopp passed without incident.

CHAPTER 10

An acquaintance I have made since I became interested in crop formations, Tom Trubridge, phoned one evening. He told me his brother Chris was interested in astronomy and, although an amateur, had made a startling discovery. One day he was looking at an Ordnance Survey map of the Avebury area. Anyone familiar with an Ordnance Survey map will automatically know that tumuli (small mounds, some of which are ancient burial sites) are marked with a very small five-pointed star symbol.

Suddenly a bell rang in his head. He had the idea to overlay a map of the stars on the Ordnance Survey map and to his astonishment they matched. When I heard about this I asked him to do a simple test using a computer program. I asked if he could run a program that would send the star system back through time, say 5,000 years, and find out when they matched perfectly.

He did this, but found no match. Then he did the same thing using a program that went back 30,000 years and still found no match. In fact the only time it does match is today. The whole object of this experiment was to see if we could date when the stones of Avebury and the tumuli were placed in their positions (see picture section).

When they only matched the position of the stars today, a chill passed through us. Had we discovered a message sent through time by the stone builders in the placement of the stones and tumuli? Could they have been saying to future generations, 'When the stars are in this position, beware,' hoping we would be intelligent enough to be able to decipher the meaning in time to avert tragedy? All the prophecies of ancient civilisations end in the year 2012. Star formations will have changed little by then.

Each year messages continue to appear in our fields. Contact is still being made. As for healing, there is strong evidence to suggest that the magnetic flux lines of our planet are breaking down, and some of the crop formations are placed on the actual break in those flux lines. We talk about the pattern of life without actually thinking about what we are saying. In actual fact everything is made of patterns. Things live in patterns, and die in patterns. You can heal using patterns.

Under an electron microscope destructive bacteria can be seen. To stop that shape being able to latch onto another and destroy it, scientists have discovered the shape of other bacteria that fit snugly onto it, which prevents it from multiplying. So one shape can destroy while another can heal.

If you get the right shape for the job, you can heal anything.

That's what I believe our friendly aliens could be doing with some crop formations. They are putting down the right shape for the job, and healing what is wrong. The magnetic flux line at Stonehenge was broken. The Julia set is a fractal geometry picture of order breaking into chaos – you could even say a picture of the way we live today. So could the Julia set be a shape that heals that breakdown? (See picture section).

The magnetic flux line at Silbury Hill was supposedly broken in 1993. Three people may have witnessed the mending of that break. They came down from Leamington because they love the area. This particular night they had walked to the top of Silbury Hill and planned to stay there all night. At around 2am it became misty but the mist was quite thin, because as the odd car went by you could see it quite clearly.

They were looking south across the A4 when one of them noticed something in the field to his left, and caught the attention of the others. All three of them say they witnessed some staggering events. They say they saw a triangular shaped orange light, and something was in the light. At first they couldn't tell what, then it became apparent it was a short, human form.

The orange triangle started to move across the road and as it did so small pinpricks of light moved away from the orange light along the ground. They described them as 'like small Christmas tree lights'. Suddenly they were aware of small beings walking on the ground with the small lights, in front of the orange light. They maintain that this continued for quite a time. They say, 'the small lights looked as though they were forming a grid'.

Then those lights were joined by another orange triangular-shaped light on the other side of the road. There was another humanoid form in that orange light. Suddenly this new orange light seemed to notice them standing there watching, and began to move across the road towards them, lifting as it did so. It stopped at their height, about 50 feet away.

For a time they stood there watching it rise and could clearly see a small being in the orange triangular light. As soon as it came level with the top of the hill where they stood, one of them took a step backwards. They felt that the orange light was mirroring this by moving away and returning to ground level. It then commenced the same procedure as the other orange light.

As they watched, they became aware of car headlights in the distance and felt that, through telepathy, they could 'hear' what was being communicated between the two orange lights and their occupants. It went something like this 'What actions shall we use to avoid the car?' It seemed as though they had several alternatives. Suddenly the two orange triangular lights came together, which made a slit of light, like when opening a fridge door about a centimetre wide. Then that slit of light reduced to a pinprick of light, and stayed that way until the car had passed. Then the slit was seen again followed by the two orange triangular lights. They then carried on in the same way as before.

They travelled across the road and up into the field directly to the south of Silbury Hill. When they neared an electricity pylon they all disappeared. The strange thing is, where those people say the light disappeared, there have been crop formations every year since. It is as though the aliens mended the flux line and then put the seal on it. Perhaps the right shapes prevent them from breaking again. They felt that the triangular orange lights were doorways of spacecraft, although they could not see the craft themselves.

Before the sceptics say 'What a load of rubbish', it should be added that a meeting took place in the Julia set formation in 1996 between Colin Andrews and a gentleman who is part of a relatively new (and at the moment secret) body of scientists, who commenced investigative work on crop formations in 1994. One of their bases is near Andover.

At the moment the Germans, English, Russians and Americans who form the project are obtaining some very interesting information about the crop formations. The gentleman that Colin spoke to says they can now distinguish which crop formations are real from those that are hoaxed. He also showed Colin a gadget that could tell how much argon gas was in the patterns.

Colin asked the gentleman who or what he believed was making the genuine crop formations. Without hesitation he said 'aliens'. He then proceeded to tell Colin what they believed was happening. The magnetic flux lines of the planet are breaking down, and in some areas of the planet it is so bad that they believe it to be irreparable. They have a colour coding system, and black is as bad as it gets.

In Czechoslovakia there has been a huge black area for many years and from there it has been getting larger and larger. It now reaches as far south as northern Spain. In the last year with the work that they have been doing at the secret base north of Andover, they have managed to bring the colour coding of Czechoslovakia up to orange. 'It is a small step but it's working slowly,' he told Colin.

Colin asked about the alien connection and was told that they are always around when there was something to know. 'When I leave here,' he told Colin, 'and go back to the base they will be waiting to see what I have discovered.' Colin hopes there will be other meetings with this gentleman, and he will help in any way he can. It's early days. With these new findings more checking has to be done, but if this turns out to be fact, at least we'll know that some secret body is doing something to help.

After Colin informed me of what this gentleman had told him, I asked a close friend to check out this base near Andover. My friend is a postman, and I figured that if anyone could get close to this base it would be a postman. As it turned out you cannot get anywhere near the place without being confronted by armed guards. 'The postman turns up at the gate and waits, and within seconds an armed guard comes and takes the letters from you,' he says. The only people with the right to be armed in this country are members of Her Majesty's Forces and the police, and they were not police.

In August 1996 I took a drive out to see the base for myself. It is bristling with closed-circuit TV cameras, and in the grounds are many new buildings which look like laboratories. What interested me more was a large earth mound in the grounds to the right of the main building. It certainly had all the hallmarks of a secret base. While we still have people like Saddam Hussein roaming the planet sure, we need to have secrets and therefore secret bases, but when it comes to space nothing should be kept from us, good or bad. We the human race have a right to know. Without taxpayers' money no one would ever have got into space. So the knowledge gained should be for the benefit of all. I for one will not rest until everything with an alien connection is common knowledge.

Throughout the years, the media has ridiculed anyone believing in UFOs. I see a time coming very soon when the media has to play catch-up. In the near future the media will be trying to discover all the intricate details of this phenomenon. Do we, who have been studying this phenomenon for many years, blame their lack of knowledge on their gullibility, the result of listening to mindless sceptics and government propaganda? Will we ever listen to the media or government again, unless there is a massive change in their perception of this subject? The answer must be no. Once we are all 100 per cent sure that the media and the government have been deceiving us on such a scale, no one can say what the result might be. Whatever the excuse the government, the Church and the media come up with, it had better be good.

The power of the mind is incredible. If we think positively, positive things will happen. Likewise if we think negatively, then negative things will happen. Collectively the human mind is a powerhouse. We can do anything we want, collectively.

Wouldn't it be great if we had a positive thought day – everybody stops for two minutes and thinks positively all over the world at the same time. Especially if we were all given the same thought to think of. I wonder what would happen. Let's say we all thought of healing the sick. I wonder. We would only have to do it once to find out if it worked. Then suppose it did, we could gradually put the whole world to rights.

It's not an impossible idea, only part of your being is in your body. The rest is an aura around it. We, like the planet, have our own space. If someone with a bad aura comes too close we move away. Someone with a good aura we allow much closer. When auras touch, you can become so close that you even know what the other is thinking. If we only think positive thoughts, and do so collectively, we could all become one for a time.

Abductees have said many times that when on board an alien craft, aliens come very close to them – eyeball to eyeball, often – and telepathy takes place. It has often been said that the eyes are the windows to the soul. Are aliens able to see into our minds?

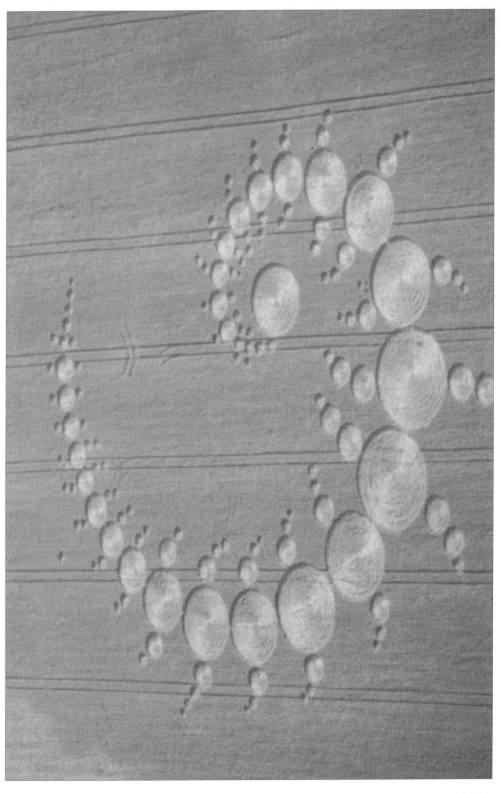

The Julia set – an image of order breaking into chaos – is this intended as a symbol of how we live today?

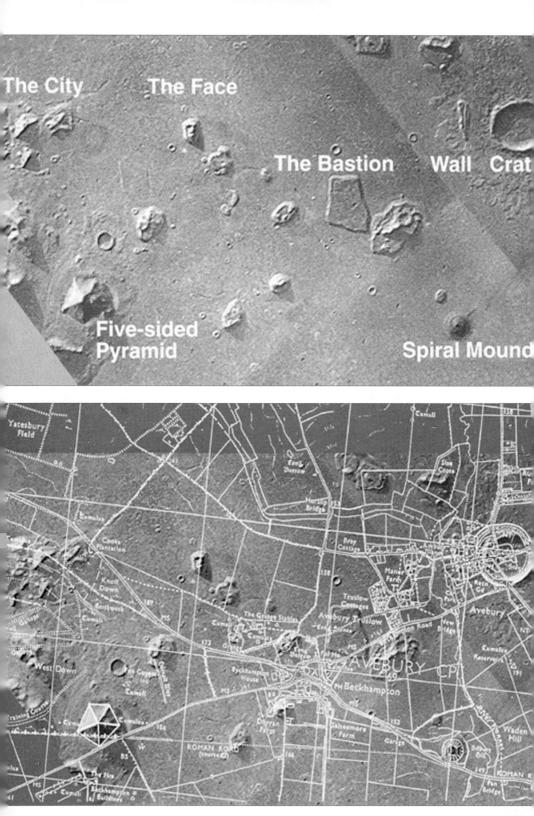

The City The Face

The Bastion Wall Crat

Five-sided
Pyramid

Spiral Mound

If the Ordnance Survey map of Avebury and the map of Cyclonid are overlaid, they correspond exactly.

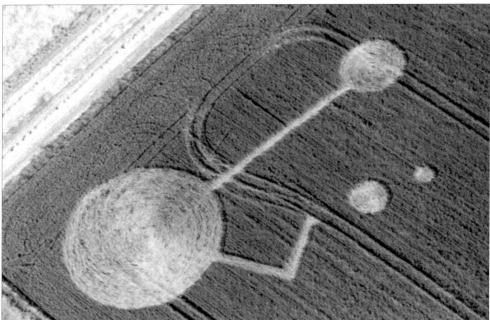

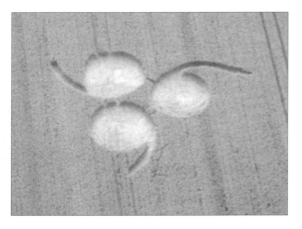

Top: Me with Colin Andrews (*left*) and Ray Santilli, at my first viewing of the alien autopsy footage.

Middle: This crop formation turned up in a field opposite Silbury Hill and shows the angle of 19.5 degrees.

Bottom left: The 'three sixes' crop formation that turned up in the same field, in East Kennet two years running.

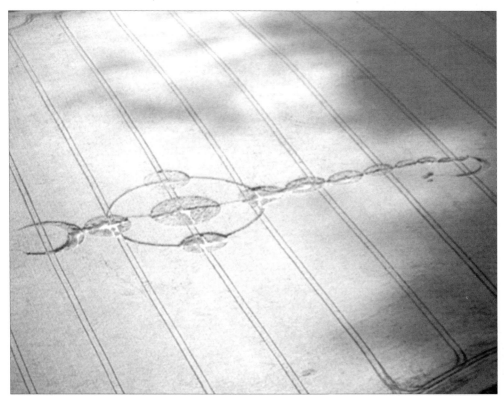

Top: The Scorpion – the pattern that Tlakaelel was searching for, even before it had been discovered!

Bottom left: My meeting at Avebury with the great Tlakaelel, the Aztec Elder, who finally reached the field of the scorpion, two years after beginning his quest for it.

Bottom right: This formation depicts our solar system, but omits the earth in it's orbit – is this a warning?

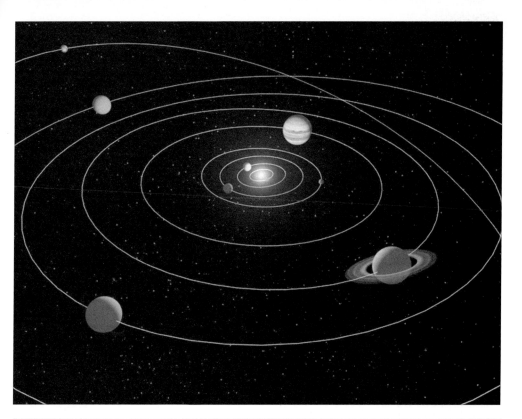

Top: Our solar system.

Bottom: Avebury Ring with the 'Spiders Web' crop formation.

Some of the most spectacular crop formations from recent years.

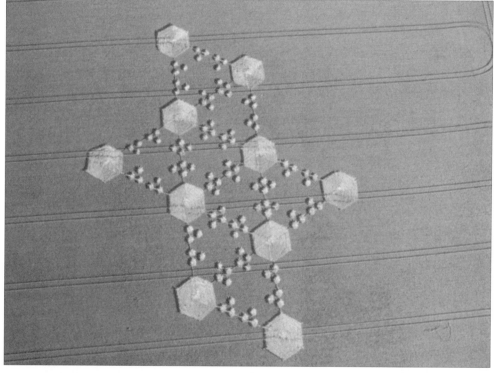

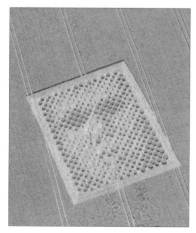

Top: Dr Rife's miraculous curing of terminally ill cancer patients made front page news.

Middle: Reg and Colin with Sergeant Brown's daughters.

Bottom right: Sergeant Brown, receiving honours from a high ranking US army official. It was later denied that he was ever in the army.

CHAPTER 11

We should always separate God and the Church. Never think of them as one and the same. The Church is a man-made business, in fact the longest running business ever, apart from prostitution, and some may argue that the latter has done more for mankind than the former.

What the Church has done in the name of God throughout history doesn't just border on the criminal, it IS criminal. The Church has killed more people than Hitler, although it has done it over a longer time period. It is largely responsible for wiping out many sophisticated cultures, including the Mayans, theAztecs and the Incas. Jesus said, 'Forgive them, oh Lord, for they know not what they do.' I say, God help them, for they *do* know what they do. As long as the Church was able to put fear of God's wrath into the people, then it was sure of its own survival.

I became aware in the 1960s that the Church owned most of the slum areas both here and around the world, but it wasn't until the 1990s that I put two and two together. I call it the sting. Here's how it works. The poor have nothing, except for their faith in God. So they go to church to pray for something better.

The Church tells them they are sinners, and must repent for their sins. Then God will forgive them, and help them. They are then told there is always someone worse off than themselves. Then after a two-hour chat show by the vicar, he sends round the poor box. The poor, for all their sins, believe the more they put in the poor box the better God will shine down on them. Woe betide anyone who puts in less than a fiver.

So the Church is robbing the poor. If God is everywhere, as the Church preaches, then you can pray anywhere. So if you're poor, pray at home – it's cheaper. The Church does not put you in touch with God, your conscience does. The Church only puts you in touch with the Church.

The Church has had it all its own way for the longest time. Only in the last few hundred years have the general public been educated enough to read. However, to read the Bible was a different story. Up until the English Authorised Version, commissioned by James 1 of England, all Bibles were written in an obscure form of church Latin. The reason for this was that if only the bishops could understand it, they could teach whatever they liked.

However if everyday folk could read it for themselves the Church's teachings would be called into question. In the early days Bible translators were condemned as heretics and would have their books burned. In 1947 a young goat herdsman discovered the Dead Sea Scrolls at Qumran. For many years after their discovery, the scrolls lay in the Vatican Vaults, and

WILD THINGS THEY DON'T TELL US

most of them are still there today. Academics who were hired to translate the scrolls had to pass all of the information to the Vatican Police before it was allowed into the public domain. These along with clay tablets found at Nag Hamadi in Egypt tell a very different story from the one that we were told.

There is no greater exponent of this work than Laurence Gardner, who has spent many years writing books on this topic. His three works on this subject are enlightening and every turn of every page is a revelation. *Bloodline Of The Holy Grail*, *Genesis Of The Grail Kings* and *Realm Of The Ring Lords* are must-reads for everyone, and the contents are of staggering importance. Not only do these books shed new light on well known figures such as Adam, Eve, Moses, Jesus and Mary Magdalene, but also the origins of elves, pixies, gnomes, goblins and the underlying stories behind fairytales such as Snow White and Cinderella.

Would you be surprised to learn that all holy men were call messiahs at the time of Christ? It was not just Jesus. Would it also surprise you to learn, that Heaven was a place which all the holy men visited from time to time, like MPs going to the Houses of Parliament. And it was not up in the clouds somewhere, but on a hill just outside Jerusalem.

I think Jesus would have been really angry if he had known we were calling his wife a prostitute. Yes, Mary Magdalene was his wife. Further, would it surprise you to know that they had three children together: Tamar, Jesus-Justus and Josephes. I must say, I was surprised to learn these things, but glad that for once, I knew the truth. No doubt about it, Jesus was a good man, and had great new ideas. He also believed women should play an integral part in religion and religious ceremonies, which

was unheard of at the time and is still frowned upon by the Catholic Church.

At least one of his so-called miracles can be laid to rest right here, when he was supposed to have changed the water into wine. This supposed miracle is meant to have occurred at the marriage feast at Canaan when Mary, Jesus' mother turned to him and said, in respect of their unsanctified guests, 'they have no wine'. Jesus having not yet been anointed to Messiah status replied, 'Mine hour is not yet come', to which Mary forced the issue. Jesus then flouted the law allowing wine for everyone. The ruler of the feast made no mention about a miracle, he was just surprised that the wine had turned up at that stage of the proceedings. Not a supernatural event as the Church would have us believe, but it was a shock at that time that someone would break with such rigid tradition.

Some people believe the marriage at Canaan to be that of Jesus and Mary Magdalene. As pointed out in *Bloodline Of The Holy Grail*, this was not the marriage ceremony itself, but a betrothal feast and as such Mary would have to have been three months pregnant. The three-month pregnancy rule stopped dynastic heirs, such as Jesus, marrying women who kept miscarrying or who proved to be barren. Perpetuation of the dynastic line was an absolute, so marriage was essential.

However, most of the so-called miracles arise from the time that Jesus met Saul on the road to Damascus. Jesus, who probably didn't realise at the time, needed a publicist and he found one, whether he liked it or not, when he met Saul. From what we can gather, Saul hated Jesus until they met, when Jesus converted Saul to Christianity. Saul, being an OTT kind of guy, just couldn't stop talking about Jesus from then on, and was responsible for telling the world about how miraculous he was.

As far as can be ascertained the Bible gospels were compiled in the 4th century but have, over the centuries, been mistranslated or deliberately amended. Jesus himself never once said he was 'the Son of God' but 'a Son of God'. All holy men called God, Father. Yet another mistake, deliberate or otherwise, by the Church. Revolutionary new ideas about religion at that time could have cost a man his life. The operative words here are 'could have'. In fact, Jesus did not die on the cross. Yes, he was crucified, but according to writings at the time, he did not die on the cross. If in English we say 'the body was taken down off the cross,' we are implying the person is dead, by the use of the word 'body'. The wrong translation from Greek to Roman was evidently responsible for this. In fact it is now popular belief among truth-seekers that he died on the borders of India and China, at the ripe old age of 73.

Information that, when missionaries visited China in the 1800s preaching the gospels, they didn't have to convert people in an area near the borders of India (because they already worshipped a man on a cross, who was not oriental), would appear to back up this theory.

The only thing Jesus could possibly be accused of is not being a very attentive husband and father. This was mainly because dynastic wedlock was quite unlike the Jewish family norm. Dynastic parents were separated at the birth of a child. Separation was for three years if it was a girl and six if it was a boy. At the end of the Bible story Jesus was expected, and became the true Messiah his people had prophesied.

However, his mission failed because the sectarian rift was too wide, and the rift is still there today. But while he went walkabout, his wife had some big decisions to make. Mary had been implicated in an uprising against the Romans and took off with her children. To save Jesus' bloodline, she fled across the Mediterranean to Gaul (France) and it was here that heirs of Mary Magdalene became the kings and queens of Europe. Hence the blue bloods, or the royal blood, or bloodline of the Holy Grail. The Holy Grail being the womb of Mary Magdalene. The cup that held the blood of Christ.

However, these were troubled times and it was not to be long before the Church sent its inquisitors in their direction. This was made possible by the Donation of Constantine. This document stated that the Emperor's Pope was Christ's elected representative on Earth with the power to create monarchs as his subordinates, while cementing the papal dignity above that of any earthly ruler.

It later emerged that this document was an outright forgery. Most amazing of all is that the document's overriding dictate is still in force today. Since then all monarchs who gained their power by church coronation and their affiliated governments have been invalid. You can now see why the Church and the thrones of Europe always worked so closely together. They were, and still are, aunts and uncles in the same business. But please, don't take my word for any of this. If you need, as I did, to know the full and intricate story to these events in our history, read *Bloodline Of The Holy Grail* by Laurence Gardner.

We, for the sake of humanity, must change this cycle of events. But not by going to war, or chopping off people's heads

– that's the old way. Today, if you think the Church or the government is wrong, you should simply ignore them. No matter what they say they will do to you, if you don't do what they tell you. Look at the poll tax situation – the people won the day. There was no real need even to go out into the streets to complain, we could have all just stayed at home and ignored what they where asking for, but kept in touch via the internet. The government would soon have got the message.

By going out on the streets to complain, you give any government the chance to twist the events to suit themselves; all they have to do is employ a few people, one short of a six pack, to make things look ugly for the cameras. Then send in the police, who are already programmed, and in the news the following day, with good editing, you're the bastards, not them.

If you're one of those people that hasn't given much thought to these things, and believes your government is an open government who will tell you everything it knows, think on this. In 1989 Colin Andrews and the CPR set up the watch called Operation Blackbird which was mentioned earlier. The media and the army were also present and everybody wanted a story – a great night for hoaxers.

In the small hours of the morning the heat-seeking cameras picked up something quite large in the field. The excitement was unbelievable, so I am told, and the media went wild. It wasn't until 15 December, 1996, at a UFO conference in Bristol, that a gentleman from a TV channel, who was there covering the event, came to Colin and I and said, 'I was at Operation Blackbird. Did you know that as soon as we picked up something on our cameras that night in the field, a D Notice was put on us all, by the government?'

To anyone not familiar with this term, it means the government does not want you, the public, to know about it. Even if they wanted to the media could not report it. As it turned out, all that was in the field that night were four hoaxers. Had it been four aliens, you and the rest of the world would never have known. When you think about that night, and the rapid response from government which supposedly doesn't believe in extra-terrestrial beings, what were they doing that night? They can't have it all ways, can they?

So you see at the moment the government can and will hide whatever they wish from us. This will change, whether the powers that be like it or not. The problems governments have are born of the fact that every government official, when voted into power, becomes full of his or her own importance, and forgets that they are there to do a job for us. We are their employers. How would the government like it if a nice tidy little UFO landed in someone's garden and was just big enough to go in the garage and they weren't told? I can assure you now, if one landed in mine they would be the last to know. The rest of the world would be first. Chance would be a fine thing.

I must say that, although I have slammed the Church and government for being ruthless and dishonest, I now believe they are mere pawns in a larger game that has been played for 6-8,000 years or more. And only the higher and more covert echelons know the rules. Governments are too transient to be trusted with the gameplan. This means we are truly fending for ourselves. Unless we, the human race, get a grip on the situation, it will go on forever.

CHAPTER 12

I must have been a teacher's nightmare when I was at school. When other children were satisfied with the teacher's answer, I was the one who asked, 'Why?' and wasn't always satisfied with the answer I got. This did not stop when I left school – it got worse. Teachers' replies were generally the stock answers that they had received when they were at school. Things change, and I, for one, needed up-to-the-minute, well-thought-out answers.

The problem is that when you leave school the first of your adult problems surfaces, the business of earning a living. That nasty five-letter word that you never really place any importance on at school rears its ugly head – money. Having to earn money puts an immediate brake on real learning, because we're forced into concentrating on learning our job so that we can feed ourselves and get from one end of the week to the other.

That, for most people, is the way it stays for the rest of their lives. Unless of course you become older, with more time on your hands, or you become a millionaire, or both. You have no time to think about the fringe elements of life or to trace them to any decent conclusions. The powers that be probably like it that way; no time to question anything.

It has been said for years that money is the root of all evil, and that's right. If it weren't for money there would be no drug problems. If people were not earning money from selling it, they would not push it. That in turn would free up our police force, because crime connected to drugs would cease. In fact, you would have no new addictions.

It might be a good idea, right now, if those in power made centres all over the country and supplied drugs for free. This would stop pushers immediately, which would prevent young people and even children getting hooked – so your six-year-old need never come into contact with drugs. For those already hooked it's too late. Let's try to save the innocent. Even judges have said this would be a good idea, so why hasn't this been implemented? The only conclusion you can draw is that people in high places would cease to make money from it.

If the government really wanted to free up the roads to stop the pollution that traffic causes, they should never have privatised the railways. If everyone in the country paid less than the cost of a TV licence the railway could be run for free, and if the railway was free, more people would use it instead of their cars.

But no, what will happen is one of two things. The government will either do as the continentals have done, and build toll booths, which will cost billions, or they will put petrol up so high that it makes the railways look cheap. Neither of these will stop pollution. It'll just mean the government will be able to thieve more money from us when we travel. And pollution will carry on getting worse.

What happened to the billions of taxpayers' money that was used to drill for the then promised oil bonanza from the North Sea? We didn't see oil prices drop! In fact we've only seen them rise. The price of oil in England is almost the highest in the world. Why? By now you're probably thinking that this is a party political broadcast on behalf of the They Screw You Out Of Everything Party. All I ask is for your patience. It all has relevance to the wider picture.

We humans, for example, have always been told that gold is a precious metal and we never question it. Why? It is not precious. It is in everything. It's even in seawater. Governments use gold to underpin their currency. Why? Startling new evidence is slowly coming to the fore that could stand the world on its head.

In the early 1900s an archaeologist called William Flinders Petrie climbed Mount Horeb in Iraq and discovered what was first thought to be a temple. Now it is believed it was where the large-scale smelting of a particular metal took place – that metal being gold. Also found at this site was a large amount of a strange white powder.

The site was thought to be at least 6-8,000 years old. Now it may be that we haven't heard about this because it doesn't fit in with the consensus of archaeologists on when man could smelt certain metals. However, it is more likely to be because of the way it was smelted. Gold melts at 1063°C. But it appears that at Mount Horeb they used heat close to the temperature of the Sun's surface – which is approximately 6,000 degrees C.

To get those kinds of temperatures 8,000 years ago was a feat in itself. But this next piece of information is mind-boggling. They were not content just to melt the gold, they went one step further and almost vapourised it. I'll explain. Today if we want to analyse a metal to find out what it consists of, it is burnt at a temperature close to that of the Sun for a period of 15 to 20 seconds. In that 20 seconds, a chart will tell the scientist exactly what elements the metal consists of. At least, that's what most scientists think.

However, buried in red tape, and only just coming to light, is the work of a Russian scientist, who asked; 'Why burn for only 15 to 20 seconds?' He then set up apparatus to burn for much longer periods. Nothing happened at 20 seconds, 30 seconds, 40 seconds, 50, 60, or 69 but at 70 seconds, the apparatus then registered elements from the palladium group – platinum and other precious metals – all from an ordinary piece of iron.

Although amazing in itself, the really incredible thing is what happens to the metal, especially when gold is melted this way. At a 70-second burn there is suddenly a bright light, like a thousand flash bulbs going off, and all that is left behind in the crucible is a white powder. The gold vanishes. Another amazing thing is that the crucible has very little weight and so does the powder. If you then take the powder out of the crucible, the weight returns to the crucible. Now I'm no scientist, but that sure sounds like what is know as 'super-conductivity' to me.

So, why did a race of people 8,000 years ago need super-conductivity? What did they need the white powder for? If a heavy stone crucible loses its weight with this white powder in it, could you put this powder on large stones and move them to build large structures with ease, perhaps while building pyramids? Pyramids are by their very name 'fire begotten', derived from the Latin word *pyre* meaning fire. To find out the answer to this question, it's perhaps better to tell you about the civilisation responsible.

It has always been assumed that the Sumerians were the first civilisation on Earth. However, since the dig at Mount Horeb by Petrie, it appears they were not. Found at the site were thousands of what looked like earthenware rolling-pins with writings around their circumferences. The writing was like no other known to man, and has taken many years to decipher. The stories they tell are chilling but also exciting. The one thing about finding pottery scrolls is that you have the master dye, unlike books, which could be changed over the years. All that was needed was for them to roll the scroll onto wet clay then decipher what they saw.

The civilisation called itself the Anunnaki. They were as civilised as we are. They had schools, lawyers, books and fashion shows. The scrolls told the story of a whole civilisation, and its way of life. The civilisation spoke of *making* Cro-Magnon man from Neanderthal man. They were not happy with the results, and their leaders argued they should destroy them, which they did by way of a great flood, saving only a few. Those who survived were bred with the Anunnaki women to make Homo Sapiens, or thinking man.

God said, 'let us make man in our image, in our likeness'. Notice a *plural* is used for God. In the Old Testament Genesis account it states, 'male and female created he them and he called their name Adam'. Older writings use the more complete name *Adama* which means 'Earthling'. The first of these beings were called Adam and Eve, then known as *Ataba* and *Khawa*. It may well be that they were bred by the Anunnaki to be the Earthly Rulers, that they were the beginning of the blood royal, the Holy Grail. Who were these people? If this is correct, no wonder they've never found the missing link.

At this point I suddenly had a thought. Why do human beings have to shield their eyes with their hand to see on a sunny day? No other animal has to squint so why do we? You don't see a horse or a cow squinting do you? A bird which flies high up in the sky where the Sun shines the brightest doesn't even use its eyelids until it goes to sleep. A polar bear doesn't suffer with snow blindness caused by the reflection of the Sun that shines even brighter with the glare. When a deer or rabbit gets caught in your car headlights, they do not even blink let alone squint. Why? Because they have adapted to living on Earth. Cro-Magnon man had a large forehead, which shielded his eyes; he would not have had to squint either. Evolution doesn't go backwards does it?

If we were from Earth we would still have a large protruding forehead to protect our eyes. Or our eyes themselves would have adapted by now. We must have come from a planet that was a little further away from its Sun. Are we the descendants of the Anunnaki?

In the Old Testament we can read stories of people living until they are 800 or 900 years old. This has been put down to translating errors by those who collated the Bible, with the Church merely saying, they meant to say 80 or 90 years old.

According to the Anunnaki, to rule over their subjects, their leaders needed longevity. Let's face it, if you get older you usually get wiser. Eight hundred years' worth is a lot of wisdom. To ensure this was the case, the Anunnaki fed their leaders bread and wine. Red wine as we know today, is very good for you; a glass a day can unclog your veins and keep them clear.

The bread the Anunnaki fed their leaders was made from a white powder made from the burning of the gold. Eating the bread made from the powdered gold, according to the Anunnaki, made their leaders more intelligent and made them live much longer.

Now the Catholic Church must have known about this, because they still give the bread and wine in their Holy Communion ceremonies. One thing we can all be sure of today, is that there will be no gold powder in their bread. We know that the last person to be fed this bread in a ceremony was the second Pharaoh. Then it stopped.

When Moses led the Jews out of Egypt, the Bible would have you believe he went up Mount Sinai and saw the burning bush and God gave him the Ten Commandments. If that were the case, he marched his people about 50 miles out of their way, and they would not have been pleased. It is more likely he went up Mount Horeb, which is en route and the story then fits what happened to him there.

The Ten Commandments were no problem for Moses. Having been brought up by a Pharaoh he would have known the inaugural ceremony of the Pharaohs, in which they had to repeat, after the high priest: 'I have not killed. I have not committed adultery.' And so on. All Moses did was change the first words to Thou shalt, instead of, I Have, and it was all over bar the carving. The ordinary Israelites would not have been aware of the inaugural words so would not have been any the wiser.

The interesting part of this is the burning bush. When you arc gold for 70 seconds at Sun temperature, it has been found that a pencil standing on its end, right next to the flash, scorches but does not fall over. What did Moses witness on top of Mount Horeb? Was it the burning of gold, when he saw the blinding light and spoke to God through the burning bush that didn't actually burn? Did Moses make a mistake and think that the Anunnaki was God or did he know the Anunnaki as his creators, so naturally thought of them as his God?

On Moses' return to his people from the Mount, he sees them worshipping a golden calf and, according to the Bible, becomes angry, burns the golden calf to dust and makes them eat it. He then smashes the tablets of stone, throws them in the Ark of the Covenant, and off they go. The Bible makes it sound as though Moses was punishing the Israelites by making them eat the calf.

It could be that he was actually turning them all into leaders. You actually smelt gold – you don't burn it. But it sounds as if that is exactly what he did. The only way of burning gold to a powder is in 70 seconds at the temperature of the Sun's surface, and only then if the gold is very thin. Otherwise you need to maintain that high temperature for 300 seconds.

It is interesting to note that the Bible puts all the emphasis on the Ten Commandments which, as we now know, were easy for Moses to create. Could the Bible be taking our attention away from the importance of the Ark of the Covenant and what it really held within? Remember it took at least four people to lift and eight to carry the Ark of the Covenant. They were told not to touch the sides, only the handles.

Did the Bible conveniently get the spelling wrong? Could it be the Arc of the Covenant? As in *electrical* arc? Is it the arc that melts the gold, with which they make the bread for higher intelligence? Is this why it's been hidden from us for thousands of years? To get the kind of temperature necessary to almost vaporise gold you would need a capacitor, and that sounds very much what the Ark of the Covenant was.

It is a fact that our brains contain a white substance. Gold is the best conductor of electricity. Our brains receive messages by electronic impulses which travel through this white substance. Scientists also know that something in your brain is super-conducting but as yet they don't know what. If we were all very intelligent, there wouldn't be any workers. We'd all be leaders.

The people responsible for putting a value on gold had to be somebody who knew gold's ultimate potential or capabilities. To the Anunnaki it was more than prized, they needed it for their way of life and probably their very existence. They could not have been from this planet, because they were too advanced for that time. So could it be they arrived from somewhere to find that the inhabitants of planet Earth are

Neanderthal – not even intelligent enough to work for them. Perhaps they then set about upgrading them to Homo Sapiens and, eventually, succeeded.

They would then have needed leaders to keep order, and perhaps they fed these leaders with the white powdered gold. The Homo Sapiens would then have been taught that gold is precious and that it needed to be mined. When the Homo Sapiens had mined it, their leaders could hoard it in vast quantities. Once the process was in motion, it would be able to run by itself. Not, perhaps, forever, but for at least a few thousand years or so. All that would be needed would be to give the Homo Sapiens a helping hand occasionally, and you would have a mining community that takes care of itself, doesn't need paying and doesn't even know who its boss is.

If you are an Anunnaki, and you live for 800 years, you don't have to wait many generations to collect your rewards. Like gathering the honey from the bees, one day the bosses will be coming back to harvest the gold, which is kept in nice convenient little heaps like at Fort Knox, ready for collection. Think about it. If you asked anybody on this planet why we prize such a common metal as gold, they could not tell you. There is no reason; most gold just sits there collecting dust.

The Anunnaki's system would continue to operate unhindered. They gave us a way of life that suited them, not necessarily us, but we knew no different. If we are looking for answers to the thousands of questions this raises, the answers have to lie with the Anunnaki themselves. Who were they? Where did they come from? And, just as important, where did they go?

They certainly existed, and we know this because of the

scrolls and their writings. Some of these are in the British Museum, along with vials of the white powder made from the gold, although the latter is not on public display. The remainder are in the Baghdad Museum which the Americans bombed during the Gulf War. By accident? I think not. To hide a secret as big as this, you have to be in complete control of the evidence. Now they are.

According to their scrolls, the Anunnaki must have had a long-term objective when they start talking about changing Neanderthal into Cro-Magnon man, then into Homo Sapiens. This is powerful stuff; this is no ordinary race of people we're talking about. We're talking about manipulating DNA. The idea of anybody knowing about such things at that time is difficult to comprehend. Then, when this race of people are successful, seeding two Homo Sapiens who they name Adam and Eve, through to Abraham, Moses and Jesus – this is mind blowing.

It is a strong possibility that the Anunnaki will soon come back for their gold. Can you imagine if the Anunnaki are doing this all round the universe? Upgrading life forms so that they can gather gold for them? Will there soon come a time when we realise that we needed the gold for our own technical evolution, and it'll be too late to save any of it?

The Europeans did the same thing to the native Americans, the native Australians, the Africans, and many others. When will we be paying them back for the gold we took? I think never. Nor will the Anunnaki be paying us back. With so many UFO sightings since the war, the Anunnaki could be here sooner rather than later.

The way all this information came to light really intrigued

me. When I first spoke to Laurence Gardner, a genealogist and author of *Bloodline Of The Holy Grail*, I was amazed to learn that the book was a by-product of his being commissioned by a European prince to trace his family tree.

He began the laborious job of tracing the Prince's ancestors back through the ages until he reached a point where he felt the need to confront the prince with the question, 'Do you know where this is all leading?' The prince asked, 'What do you mean?' Laurence replied, 'Do you realise your family lineage goes back to Jesus?' to which the royal replied, 'Oh yes I knew that, I just wanted to know how it got there.' Laurence replied, 'Well, I'm sure not many people know this.' What the Royal took for granted, we mere mortals knew nothing about.

When Laurence had finished the work for the Royal he decided to write the book. However he became so intrigued by his findings he could not stop at that, and carried on investigating Jesus' bloodline, and produced his second book, *Genesis Of The Grail Kings*, which led a trail through from Jesus to Moses, Abraham and Adam and Eve.

An interesting point that this raises is that the Bible states that Jesus' father Joseph was a carpenter. However, this is not what the original text of the Bible states. What was actually said was that Joseph was a Master of the Craft. Anyone who knows a little of modern Freemasonry will know the term 'the craft' and it has nothing to do with wood.

What the Bible was actually telling us (before the Church got hold of it) was that Joseph was just one of a long line of highly trained metallurgists. The only people that could be metallurgists at that time were priests and royalty and you would need to be a metallurgist to be able to convert gold into white powder.

To add more weight to Laurence's work (if that's possible) is the work of the pioneering researcher David Hudson, an American dirt farmer. Now according to David, the difference between dirt farmers and ordinary farmers is that the dirt farmer has to make his own soil from pulverising rock. In 1975 he was doing an analysis of natural products in the area where he was farming. David explains:

'You have to understand that in agriculture, in the state of Arizona we have a problem with sodium soil. This high-sodium soil, which looks like chocolate ice cream on the ground, is just crunchy black. It crunches when you walk on it. Water will not penetrate this soil. Water will not leech the sodium out of the ground. It's called black alkali.'

David was aware that it was possible to leech the sodium from the soil with sulphuric acid. Neighbouring his farm was a copper mine whose waste product was sulphuric acid. He was able to obtain as much as he needed as long as he moved it himself. He eventually administered between 30–60 tons per acre over his land. This penetrated 3 or 4 inches into the ground. When he irrigated, the soil would froth and foam due to the action of the sulphuric acid. What it did was to change black alkali into white alkali, which was water-soluble.

Within two years he was able to grow crops. Evidently it is very important to have enough calcium in the soil in the form of calcium carbonate. Calcium carbonate will act as a buffer for the acid in the soil. If you do not have enough calcium, the acidity in the soil goes down. You get a pH of 4 to 4.5 and it ties up all the trace nutrients. That being the case the cotton plant would come out of the ground and suddenly stop growing. David said, 'It is important when you are putting all these amendments to your soil that you understand what is in your soil, how much iron there is, how much calcium and so on.'

In doing the analysis of these natural products David was coming across a material consisting of no one knew quite what. It seemed more abundant in one area so they decided to begin there. Using chemistry he dissolved the material in a solution and it became blood red. Yet when he precipitated this material out chemically by using a reductant of powdered zinc, the material would come out as a black precipitant just like it was supposed to if it were a 'noble' element. With a noble element, if you chemically bring it out of acid, it won't re-dissolve in the acid.

After he precipitated this material out of the black he took the material and dried it. At the time David had no drying furnace so he just took it outside in the warm Arizona sunshine which, he says, was 115 degrees at 5 per cent humidity, so it really dried fast. Then a strange thing happened.

After the material dried, it exploded. But this was no normal explosion. It just went poof! It was neither an explosion, nor an implosion; all the material had gone in a flash as if 50,000 flash bulbs had gone off all at one time. So David took a new pencil and stood it on end next to the material as it was drying. When the material detonated, it burned the pencil about 30 per cent but did not knock the pencil over. Whatever this stuff was, David thought, it was wild.

He discovered if he dried the material away from sunlight, it did not explode. He then took some of the powder that had dried away from the sunlight, and using a crucible reduction vessel made of porcelain, he mixed the powdered material with lead and flux, and heated it until the lead melted.

When you do this, the metals that are heavier than lead stay in the lead and those that are lighter float out. This is a tried-and-tested way of doing metals analysis.

This material settled to the bottom of the lead just as if it was gold and silver. It seemed to be denser than lead and it was separated from it. Yet when he took this material and put it on a bone ash cupel, the lead soaked into the cupel and left a bead of gold and silver. He then took this bead of gold and silver for analysis to all the commercial laboratories and they said, 'Dave, there is nothing there but gold and silver'.

The strange thing was, Dave could take the bead and hit it with a hammer and shatter it, like glass. There is no known alloy of gold and silver that is not soft. Gold and silver dissolve in each other readily and form a solid solution. Both are soft elements so any alloy made from them will be soft and ductile. If you hit gold and/or silver with a hammer it will flatten out like a pancake. David told them, 'Something's going on here that we don't understand. Something unusual is happening.'

David took the beads of gold and silver back to his laboratory and separated them chemically. All he had left was a quantity of black stuff. He then took this back to the commercial laboratories and they told him it was iron, silica and aluminium. He told them it couldn't be iron, silica and aluminium. Firstly you can't dissolve it in any acids or any bases once it is totally dry. It doesn't dissolve in fuming sulphuric acid, it doesn't dissolve in sulphuric nitric acid, and it doesn't dissolve in hydrochloric nitric acid. Even gold dissolves in that, yet it won't dissolve this black stuff.

David decided to hire a PhD at Cornell University who considered himself an expert on precious elements. He paid the doctor to go to Arizona to see the problem for himself. He told David he had a machine back at Cornell that could analyse down to parts per billion. He said, 'If you let me take this material back to Cornell I'll tell you exactly what you have, if it's anything above iron we will find it.'

When they arrived back and tested the material he told David, 'You have iron, silica and aluminium.' David asked, 'Can we borrow a chemistry laboratory?' The doctor told him there was one not being used and together they spent the rest of the day there. They were able to remove all of the silica, all of the iron and all of the aluminium. Yet they still had 98 per cent of the sample that was pure nothing.

By now, more than a little frustrated, David said, 'I can hold this in my hand, I can weigh it, I can perform chemistry with it. That has to be something. It is not nothing.' The doctor told David if he would give him US$350,000 dollars as a grant he would get graduate students to look into it. David had already paid him US$22,000, because he said he could analyse anything, and he hadn't. Neither had he offered to pay David back. So David said, 'I don't know what you pay people around here, but I pay minimum wages on the farm and get a whole lot more out of US$350,000 than you can. So I'm going back to do the work myself.'

He went back to Phoenix totally disillusioned with

academia. He was neither impressed with the PhDs or the money they charged. He discovered whilst at Cornell that they work students to generate papers, but the papers say nothing. The government however pays them for every paper they write, so they get their money based on the amount of papers they turn out. They all say the same thing: they just reword it and turn out another paper.

David was in no way about to give in, and began asking around the Phoenix area where he found a man who was a spectroscopist who had studied in West Germany at the Institute for Spectroscopy. He had also been a technician for a Lab Test company in Los Angeles, which actually built spectroscopic equipment.

He was also the man who blueprinted the machines, and designed them, constructed them, then took them to the field and made them work. David thought, here is a good man. This is not just a technician. Here is a man who knows how the machine works. Around this time, David had obtained a Soviet book entitled, *The Analytical Chemistry of the Platinum Group Elements* by Ginzburg, et al. The Soviet Academy of Science published it. David continues:

'In this book, according to the Soviets, you had to do a 300-second burn on these elements to read them. For those who have never performed spectroscopy, it involves taking a carbon electrode that is cupped at the top. You then put the powder on that electrode; you bring the other electrode down above it, which creates an arc. In about 15 seconds, the carbon at this high temperature burns away, the electrode's gone and your sample's gone. All normal laboratories in the USA and possibly right around the world are doing this, then giving a full and final result after only a 15 second burn.

'According to the Soviet Academy of Sciences, the boiling temperature of water is to the boiling temperature of iron just as the boiling temperature of iron is to the boiling temperature of these elements. As you know from driving a car, as long as there is water in the motor of your car the temperature of the car engine will never get hotter than the temperature of water. If you just heated the water on the stove in a pan, you know that the pan never gets hotter than the boiling temperature of water until the water is gone. Once all the water is gone, the temperature skyrockets very fast.

'As long as there is iron there, the temperature of the sample can never get hotter than the boiling temperature of the iron, so you can then heat this stuff. Now, it is hard to fathom how something with as high a temperature as iron could be just like water to these elements, but it is.

'So we had to design and build an excitation chamber where argon gas could be put around this electrode so that no oxygen or air could get into the carbon electrode and we could burn it not for 15 seconds but for 300 seconds. According to the Soviet Academy of Sciences, this is the length of time we had to burn the sample.

'We set up, we got the Pk blenders, we got the standards, we modified the machine, we did all the analysis for results, we did all the spectral lines on this three-and-a-half-metre instrument. It was a huge machine. It took up the whole garage area. It was about 30 feet long and about 8 or 9 feet high.

'Anyway, when we ran this material, during the first 15

seconds we got iron, silica, and aluminium, little traces of calcium and sodium, maybe a little titanium now and then, and then it went quiet and nothing read. So, at the end of 15 seconds, we were getting nothing. Twenty seconds, 25 seconds, 30 seconds, 35 seconds, 40 seconds – still nothing. Forty-five seconds, 50 seconds, 55 seconds, 60 seconds, 65 seconds, but if you looked in through the coloured glass, sitting there on the carbon electrode was this little ball of white material. There was still something in there.

'At 70 seconds, exactly when the Soviet Academy of Sciences said it would read, palladium began to read. And after the palladium, platinum began to read. After the platinum, rhodium began to read. After rhodium, ruthenium began to read. After the ruthenium, then iridium began to read and after the iridium, osmium began to read.

'Now, if you're like me, I didn't know what these elements were. I had heard of platinum, but what were these other elements? Well, there are six platinum group elements in the periodic table, not just platinum. They didn't find out about them at the same time, so they have been added one at a time.

'They are all elements: ruthenium, rhodium and palladium are light platinum. Well, we came to find out that rhodium was selling for about US$3,000 per ounce. Gold sells for about US$400 an ounce. Iridium sells for about US$800 an ounce. Then you say to yourself "Gee, these are important materials, aren't they?" They are important materials because the best known deposits in the world are now being mined in South Africa.

'In this deposit you have to go half a mile into the ground

and mine an 18-inch seam of this stuff. When you bring it out, it contains one-third of one ounce per ton of all the precious elements. We checked our analysis, which we ran for two-and-a-half years, over and over. We checked every spectral line. We checked every potential on interference; we checked every aspect. We wanted exact matches.

'When we were finished, the man was able to do quantitative analysis, and he said "Dave, you have 6 to 8 ounce per ton of palladium, 12 to 13 ounces per ton of platinum, 150 ounces per ton of osmium, 250 ounces per ton of ruthenium, 600 ounces per ton of iridium, and 800 ounces per ton of rhodium, or a total of 2,400 ounces per ton, when the best-known deposit in the world is one-third of one ounce per ton."

'This work wasn't an indication that these elements were there. These elements were there and they were there in *beaucoup* amounts. They were saying, "Hey stupid man, pay attention! We are trying to show you something." If they had been there in little amounts, I probably would have been content with this. But they were there in such huge amounts, I said, "Golly, how can they be there in these quantities and no one knew it?"

'Now, you keep in mind, it wasn't one spectral analysis! It was two-and-a-half years of spectral analysis, running this material every day. And the man actually sent me away when they read because he could not believe it either. He worked on it another two months before he called me up and said, "Dave, you are right". That is how sceptical he was about it. He couldn't apologise to me. He is a German researcher with German pride, so he had his wife call and apologise to me.

'He was so impressed that he went back to Germany to the

Institute of Spectroscopy. He was actually written up in the spectroscopic journals as having proven the existence of these elements in natural materials in the south-western United States. They're not the kind of journals that you and I would ever get to read, but I actually saw the journals and he was written up.

'They had no idea where this stuff was coming from, how we were producing it, what concentrations we had gone through or anything. They had analysed just this small amount of powder. The crazy thing about it was that all we had done was to remove the silica and send the other stuff in.

'They were pretty unbelievable numbers. After we had come at this in every way we knew, in order to disprove it, I decided all we had to do was throw money at this problem, because money solves everything, right? So, at 69 seconds, I stopped the burn. I let the machine cool down and I took a pocket knife and dug that little bead out of the top of the electrode. When you shut off the arc, it absorbs down into the carbon and you have to dig down into the carbon to get the little bead of metal.

'So I sent this little bead of metal over to Harwell Laboratories near Oxford in England. They made a precious metal analysis of this bead. I got a report back: "No precious elements detected." Now this was one second before the palladium was supposed to start leaving. Yet, according to neutron activation, which analysed the nucleus itself, there were no precious elements detected. This made absolutely no sense at all. There had to be an explanation here. Either this material had been converted to another element or it was in a form that we didn't understand yet. So I decided I had to get more information on it.

'I went to a PhD analytical chemist, John Sickafoose, a man trained in separating and purifying individual elements out of unknown material. He was trained at Iowa State University and had a PhD in metal separation systems. He's the man that Motorola and Sperry used in the State of Arizona to handle their wastewater problems. He has worked with all the rare earths, he has worked with all the man-made elements.

'He has physically separated everything on the periodic table with the exception of four elements. Coincidentally, I went to him to have him separate six elements; four of those were the elements he had never worked on. He said "You know, Mr Hudson, I have heard this story before. All my life – and I'm a native Arizonan, too – I heard this story about these precious elements.

'"I am very impressed with the way you have gone about this, with the systematic way you have approached it. I cannot accept any money because if I accept money from you I have to write you a written report. All I have to sell is my reputation. All I have to sell is my credibility. I'm a certified expert witness in the state of Arizona in metallurgical separation systems."

'He said, "Dave, I will work for you for no charge until I can show you where you are wrong. When I can tell you where you are wrong, I'll give you a written report. Then you will pay me US$60 an hour for the time I spent." This would have come to about US$12,000 to US$15,000 dollars. If this got rid of the curse, if this just got the thing answered once and for all, it would be worth it. Do it, get on with it.

'Well, three years later, he said, "I can tell you it is not any of the other elements on the periodic table. We are educated; we are taught to do the chemical separation of the material and then send it for instrumental confirmation."

'The example I use is rhodium because it has a unique colour in the chloride solution. It is a cranberry colour, almost like the colour of grape juice. There is no other element that produces the same colour in chloride solution. When my rhodium was separated from all the other elements, it produced that colour of chloride.

'The last procedure you do to separate the material out is to neutralise the acid solution, and it precipitates out of solution as a red-brown dioxide. It is heated under a controlled atmosphere to 800 degrees for an hour, and that creates the anhydrous dioxide. Then you hydro-reduce that under a controlled atmosphere to get the element, and then you anneal away the excess hydrogen.

'So, we neutralised the acid solution and precipitated it out as a red-brown dioxide, which is the colour it is supposed to precipitate out at. Then we filtered that out. We heated it under oxygen for an hour in a tube furnace, then we hydro-reduced it to this grey-white powder, exactly the colour rhodium should be as an element. Then we heated it up to 1,400 degrees under argon to anneal away the material, and it turned snow-white. Now this wasn't expected. This just isn't what is supposed to happen.

'What John did was, he said, "Dave, I'm going to heat it to the anhydrous dioxide. I'm going to cool it down. I'm going to take one third of the sample and put it into a sealed vial. I'm going to put the rest of the sample back onto the tube furnace and heat it up under oxygen, cool it back down, purge it with inert gas, and heat it back up under hydrogen to reduce away the oxides.

'"The hydrogen reacts with the oxygen, forming water, and cleans the metal. I'll cool that down to the grey-white powder. I'll cool down that grey-white powder. I'll take half of that and put it into another sealed vial. I'll take the rest of the powder and put it back into the furnace. I'm going to oxidise it, hydro-reduce it and anneal it to the white powder. Then I will put it into a vial and send all three vials to Pacific Spectrochem over in Los Angeles, one of the best spectroscopic firms in the U.S."

'The first analysis came back: the red-brown dioxide was iron oxide. The next material came back: silica and aluminium: no iron present. Just putting hydrogen on the iron oxide had made the iron quit being iron, and now it had become silica and aluminium.

'Now, this was a big sample. We'd just made the iron turn into silica and aluminium. The snow-white annealed sample was analysed as calcium and silica. Where had the aluminium gone? John said, "Dave, my life was so simple before I met you. This makes absolutely no sense at all."

'He said, "What you are working with is going to cause them to rewrite physics books, rewrite chemistry books and come to a completely new understanding." John gave me the bill: it was US$130,000, which I paid. But he said, "Dave, I have separated it physically and I have checked it chemically 50 different ways. You have 4 to 6 ounces per ton of palladium, 12 to 14 ounces per ton of platinum, 150 ounces per ton of osmium, 250 ounces per ton of ruthenium, 600 ounces per ton of iridium,

800 ounces per ton of rhodium."

'These were almost the exact same numbers that the spectroscopist had told me were there. It was such an incredible number that John said, "Dave, I've got to go to the natural place where this stuff comes from and I've got to take my own samples."

'So he went up and actually walked the property and took his own samples, put them in a bag, brought them back to the laboratory, pulverised the entire sample and then started doing the analysis on what is called the master blend sample. This represents the whole geology, and he got the same numbers.

'We worked on this from 1983 until 1989, one PhD chemist, three master chemists, and two technicians working full-time. Using the Soviet Academy of Sciences' and the US Bureau of Standards' weights and measures information as a starting point, we literally learned how to do qualitative and quantitative separations of all these elements.

'We learned how to take commercial standards and make them disappear. We learned how to buy rhodium trichloride, as the metal, from Johnson, Matthey & Engelhardt and we learned how to break all these metal-metal bonding until it was literally a red solution but no rhodium was detectable. And it was nothing but pure rhodium from Johnson, Matthey & Engelhardt.

'We learned how to do it with iridium, we learned how to do it with gold, we learned how to do it with osmium, and we learned how to do it with ruthenium. This is what we found when we actually purchased a machine for high-pressure liquid chromatography.

'For your information, this person named John Sickafoose

was the man who actually wrote his PhD thesis at Iowa State University on how to build this instrument back in 1963–64. After he graduated, some of the graduate students there took that technology and developed it, and eventually Dow Chemical came in and bought it.

'Dow went ahead and commercialised it, and now it is the most sophisticated chemical separation instrument that the world has. It's computer-controlled, all high-pressure, and you can do very precise separations with it. Because this is the man who conceptualised and designed it and told them what the limitations would eventually be on it, he was the ideal man to take the technology and perfect it.

'So we were able to use their basic technology and develop a separation system for the rhodium trichloride. We actually separated five different species in the commercial rhodium trichloride. The word "metal" is like the word "army". You can't have a one-man army. The word metal refers to a conglomerate material.

'It has certain properties: electrical conductivity, heat conduction, and all these other aspects. When you dissolve the metals in acid, you get a solution that is clear without solids. You assume it's a free-ion solution, but when you are dealing with noble elements they're still not free ions. It's what is called "cluster chemistry".

'Since the 1950s there has been a whole area of research in colleges on cluster chemistry and catalytic materials. But what happens is that the metal-metal bonds are still retained by the material. So, if you buy rhodium trichloride from Johnson, Matthey & Engelhardt, you are actually getting $Rh12Cl36$ or

Rh15Cl45. You really aren't getting RhCl3. There is a difference between the metal-metal bonding material and the free ions. What you are buying is cluster chemistry; you are not getting free ions. When you put the material in for the instrumentation to analyse, it is actually the metal-metal bonds of the cluster that are analysed. The instrumentation is not really analysing the free ions.

'I heard that General Electric was building fuel cells using rhodium and iridium. So I made contacts with the fuel cell people back in Massachusetts and travelled there to meet with them. They had three attorneys meet with us, and the GE people were also there.

'The attorneys were there to protect the GE people because a lot of people say they have technologies and they meet with them; then after the meeting they sue them, claiming that GE stole their technology. Then to defend themselves, GE has to divulge what their technology really is. So GE is very sceptical when you say that you have something new. They bring their high-faluting attorneys to really screen you.

'After about an hour they said, "These guys are for real. You attorneys can leave." That was because they had also had the explosions. They knew that when they buy the commercial rhodium trichloride it analyses very well. But to make it ready to go into their fuel cells they have to do salt effusions on it, where they melt the salt and put the metal in with it to disperse it further. They know that when they do that, the metal doesn't analyse as well any more. So when we told them we had material that didn't analyse at all, they couldn't conceive how this was possible. They had never seen it, but they said, "We are interested".

'Now the GE are the people who build analytical instrumentation! They said, "Dave, why don't you just make a bunch of rhodium for us and send it to us and we'll mount it in our fuel-cell technology. We'll see if it works in places where only rhodium works. What is the mechanism of conversion of monatomic rhodium to metallic rhodium in these fuel cells? No other metal has ever been found which will perform the catalysis in the hydrogen-evolving technology of the fuel cell, other than rhodium and platinum. And rhodium is unique compared to platinum because rhodium does not poison with carbon monoxide and platinum does.

'They said, "Dave, we'll just run it to see if it's a hydrogen-evolving catalyst and, if it is, then we will see if it is carbon monoxide-stable and, if it is, then it's rhodium or it's a rhodium alternative."

'So we worked for about six months and refined that amount of material and we re-refined it and re-refined it. We wanted to be absolutely sure that this was really clean stuff. We didn't want any problems with this. We sent it back to Tony LaConti at GE. GE, who by that time had sold their fuel-cell technology. All the GE fuel-cell people had gone to work for United Technologies, and, since United Technologies already had their in-house people, the GE people were not integrated into the existing teams. So all the GE people were junior people; they weren't senior any more. After a certain period of months they all quit and left United Technologies.

'Well, Jose Giner, who was the head of fuel-cells at United Technologies, also quit and went to set up his own firm, called

Giner Incorporated, in Waltham, Massachusetts. Tony and all the GE people went with him. By the time our material got there, they'd set up their own company in Waltham, so we contracted with them to build the fuel cells for us.

'When our material was sent to them, the rhodium, as received, was analysed as not having any rhodium in it. Yet when they mounted it on carbon in their fuel-cell technology and ran the fuel cell for several weeks, it worked and did what only rhodium would do, and it was carbon monoxide-stable. After three weeks, they shut down the fuel cells, took out the electrodes and sent them back to the same place that said there was no rhodium in the original sample.

'Now there was over 8 per cent rhodium in the original sample. What happened was it had begun to nucleate on the carbon! It actually had begun to grow metal-metal bonds! So now there was metallic rhodium showing on the carbon, where before there was no rhodium.

'These GE people said, "Dave if you are the first one to discover this, if you are the first one to explain how to make it in this form, if you are the first one to tell the world that it exists, then you can get a patent on this." I said, "I'm not interested in patenting this." Then they told me that if someone else discovered it and patented it, even though I was using it every day, they could stop me from doing it. I said, "Well, maybe I should patent it."

'So in March 1988, we filed US and worldwide patents on Orbital Rearranged Monatomic Elements. Now that is a mouthful, so, to make it short, we called it ORMEs. You have ORMEs gold, ORMEs palladium, ORMEs iridium, ORMEs ruthenium, ORMEs osmium. While we were doing this patent procedure, the Patent Office said, "Dave, we need more precise data, we need more exact data, we need more information about this conversion to this white powder state."

'One of the problems we had was that when you make this white powder and you bring it out into the atmosphere, it really starts gaining weight. I'm not talking about a little bit of weight, I'm talking about 20 to 30 per cent. Now that normally would be called absorption of atmospheric gases: the air is reacting with it and causing weight gain, but not 20 to 30 per cent.

'Nonetheless, we had to answer the Patent Office. We had to come up with exact data for the Patent Office. So what we did was use this machine for thermogravimetric analysis. This is a machine that has total atmospheric control of the sample. You can oxidise it, hydro-reduce it, and anneal it, while continually weighing the sample under a controlled atmosphere. Everything is all sealed. We were getting short of funding and couldn't afford to buy one, so we leased one from the Bay Area from Varian Corporation. They sent it in to us and we set it up on computer controls.

'We heated the material at 1.2 degrees per minute and cooled it at 2 degrees per minute. What we found was that when you oxidise the material, it weighs 102 per cent; when you hydro-reduce it, it weighs 103 per cent. So far, so good. No problem. But, when it turns snow white, it weighs 56 per cent! Now that's impossible! When you anneal it and it turns white, it only weighs 56 per cent of the beginning weight! If you put that on a silica test boat and you weigh it, it weighs 56 per cent! If you heat it to the point that it fuses into the glass, it turns black and all the weight returns. So the material hadn't volatilised away. It was still there. It just couldn't be weighed any more.

'That's when everybody said, "This just isn't right; it can't be!" Do you know that we heated it, and cooled it, and heated it and cooled it, and heated it and cooled it under helium or argon? When we cooled it, it would weigh 300 to 400 per cent of its beginning weight; when we heated it, it would actually weigh less than nothing? If it wasn't in the pan, the pan would weigh more than the pan weighs when this stuff is in it! Keep in mind, these are highly trained people running this instrumentation, and they would come in and say, "Take a look at this. This makes no sense at all!"

'Now, this machine is so precisely designed and controlled that they have a magnetic material they can put into this that is non-magnetic when it goes into the machine but at 300 degrees it becomes magnetic. It is in fact a strong magnet. Then, after you get up to 900 degrees, it loses its magnetism. You can actually see if the interaction of the magnetism with the magnetic field of the heating element causes any change in weight.

'The heating element is bifilar-wound. This means that it goes round and round the sample; then you reverse it and wind it right back up so all the current runs against itself all the time. So when a wire flows electricity there is a magnetic field that forms around it, but when you run the wire right next to it, going in the other direction, it forms a magnetic field in the other direction. The idea is that the two fields will cancel. This is the kind of wiring that is used in television to cancel all the magnetic fields. The designers of this machine wanted to eliminate the magnetic field aspect here.

'When we put the magnetic material in the sample and ran it in the machine, there was no response at all. There was no change in weight when the material became magnetic or lost its magnetism. Yet when our material was put in there and it turned white, it went to 56 per cent of its beginning weight. If you shut off the machine and let it cool, it was exactly 56 per cent. If you heated it, it would go less than nothing, and if you cooled it, it would go 300 to 400 per cent, but it always went back to a steady 56 per cent.

'We contacted Varian in the Bay Area and said, "Look, this just doesn't make any sense. There's something wrong with this machine, something isn't right. Every time we use the machine it works fine unless we make the pure monatomic material, and when we do, it turns snow-white and doesn't work correctly any more." Varian looked over our results and said, "You know, Mr Hudson, if you were working with the cooling of the material we would say it is super-conducting. But inasmuch as you are heating the material, we don't know what you've got."

'I decided, well, I have had to learn chemistry and I've had to learn physics, and now I've got to learn the physics of super-conductors. So I bought and borrowed a bunch of graduate books on super-conductivity and I began to read about super-conductors.'

'Evidently there are several phenomena which occur. We hooked a voltmeter (used for checking circuitry) up to the white powder expecting the needle to leap across the voltmeter because this was supposed to be perfect conductivity, but nothing happened. Instead of this being a perfect conductor of electricity it's a perfect insulator.

'So we went back to the book for more information, and discovered that super-conductivity by definition will not allow any voltage potential to exist inside the sample. Now to get the electricity off the wire and into the sample takes a voltage potential, likewise to get electricity out of the sample and on to the wire needs a voltage potential.

'Yet by definition a super-conductor does not allow any voltage potential to exist in the sample. So we thought, What good is this? But what you learn is that you must resonance-frequency tune the vibration frequency of the electron wave, until the vibrational frequency of the electron wave is perfectly matched with the vibrational frequency wave of the super-conductor.

'Then the electrons will go on with no push at all because they are seeking the path of least resistance and that is in the super-conductor. When you do get them matched up, a strange thing happens when they go onto the super-conductor; the electrons pair up. They don't go on as individual electrons they go on in pairs! They go on as light.

'Now a curious thing happens, an electron has mass and it exists in space-time, you cannot have two electrons in the same space-time, it won't happen. They exist in different places and locations, but when they pair up and become light you can put billions of them in the same space-time.

'So now what happens with a super-conductor, as long as the frequency electron wave matches the frequency of the super-conductor, is that they keep going onto the super-conductor, more and more and more and more, you don't have to take them off, because they are going on as light. And the only way you know they are in there is by checking the size of the Mizner-field that forms around the super-conductor.

'So what is a Mizner-field? Well, when electricity flows through a wire it produces a magnetic field around the wire, but with a super-conductor it produces what they call a Mizner-field. The cool thing about this is that it does not produce a north and south pole. It's a null field. A super-conductor has no resistance, so you could keep putting energy into it, to the point where it has so much Mizner field around it that it becomes larger and larger, because of all the electrons and amperage.

'It will then begin to float on the Earth's magnetic field. It will cause the Earth's magnetic field to travel around it; it will not enter into the sample. It will become stuck in the magnetic field it is sitting in. To a point, you can put, as much energy in a super-conductor as you like, before it becomes HC2, which is a critical mass where as it becomes so huge it collapses and becomes normal. You don't want to be around when this happens.

'To get the energy out of a super-conductor you put the wire up to it and resonance frequency tune the vibration frequency of the wire to match the super-conductor and apply a voltage potential and it comes out. The neat thing is you can make a super-conductor that say runs from Tampa to San Francisco and you can resonance frequency tune the energy, put it in the super-conductor here, and it will get a free ride all the way to San Francisco. All these atoms in perfect resonance harmony producing a quantral wave, and the energy gets on this wave system and has a free ride all the way to San Francisco.'

At this point, while David goes on to talk about the possibility of floating trains, which they already have in Japan but which work by using opposing magnetic fields, I was imagining a huge egg-shaped craft with Dave's super-conductive powder sandwiched in-between an outer skin with people inside ready to go to Australia at the speed of light. Because if Earth's gravitational field has no effect on the occupants because of the Mizner field, speed would not be a problem. Perhaps even to the Moon and beyond. Travel would become so quick and easy. David continued:

'In March 1988 we filed worldwide patents and US on Orbital Rearranged Monatomic Elements, ORMES. Each element had individual patents. You can imagine the patent office when we tried to patent gold, oh great, who are these guys? Then I filed another set of patents on the super-conductive state. Which is a resonance couple system of quantum oscillators, so there had to be a many atom state of ORMES so we had to call it S- ORMES. The super-conducting state.

'You can have a patent on the atom but you also have to have a patent on the systems of atoms. It's like a man being an army, a man can't be an army, a one-man army isn't real, an army is many men. Well a super-conductor is many atoms, you can't have one atom being a super-conductor. So we had to have a patent on ORMES and a patent on S-ORMES.

'Well I didn't know that the law said that any patent involving super-conductivity has to have the approval of the

Department of Defence, because of the strategic interest of the government. I didn't know this, so I just went ahead and filed the patent. Well, the Department of Defence didn't get involved. I only used the word super-conductivity once in the closing paragraph on the summary page of my patent application.

'I said it has horns, it has four hooves, it moos, it gives milk, it has baby calves, but I didn't use the word cow. I talked about the Mizner field, its reaction with gravity (the levitation), but I didn't use the word super-conductivity except one time in the closing paragraph. So they never realised it was a super-conducting patent.

'By law you have one year's grace, from when you file a US patent, to file a worldwide patent. So I waited until about three weeks before the end of the year, and contacted the patent office and told them I'm going to file a worldwide patent. Evidently, someone at the patent office re-read my patent application again and said, "Oh gosh it's about super-conductivity."

'Off to the Department of Defence it went, back it came and it said, "He cannot file worldwide". Then I went back to them and said, "Wait, by law I have a six month appeal period, I've only got three weeks. So they over-rode the Department of Defence, and let me file worldwide.

'Now needless to say by now my name was mud at the Department of Defence. Next, I get a phone call from this guy out of the blue, who wants to invest in my technology. I said, "How did you hear about this?" he said, "Well, everybody's talking about it."

'Anyhow, he's telling me about things that nobody should know, he's quoting specific references out of my patent, and nobody is supposed to have seen this, except the patent office and the military review board. So I had a private investigator check him out; I said "Find out who he is and where he comes from."

'We found out he flies out of Langley airforce base, he gets his money from a Swiss bank account that the military keeps stocked with money and his job is to provide money to companies whose technologies they need for Star Wars. When they took this legislation to the legislator here in the United States, they turned it down. They didn't allow funding money for Star Wars.

'So what the military does is put money in Swiss bank accounts that nobody knows about, and this investor goes around looking for companies that need support and when he finds them he funnels money into those companies.'

He said to Dave, 'I've got to have this stuff, because the only way you're going to get absolute confirmation that no one will question, is to have it show that it reflects neutrons.' He went on to say, 'I can get you on line for this in a couple of weeks, whereas it will take you three years.' Dave said, 'Then I'll wait three years.'

He said, 'Dave, have you ever taken this to a university and had university funding or government funding or grants of any kind?' Dave said, 'no'. There was just no way they could get involved with him legally. Dave said, 'he came back to me a couple of times and then gave up'. There was no way he could make Dave do anything. He could see he was totally private and there was nothing he could do.

When you understand that this produces gamma radiation,

the last thing you need is the military having this information. However, before they let Dave go to patent pending in the US, the military had to approve it. They told him, 'You must get this confirmed by a totally independent laboratory, someone who has no affiliation with you, someone with credentials.' So he told them how about Argon National Laboratories. Were they good enough?

'Yes they're a government laboratory,' they said. 'OK, so we'll have it done by them,' Dave said. So they said, 'Here's what we want you to do, we want you to buy pure yellow gold, 999.99 per cent pure gold, and convert it into white powder, and if you can do that, we'll let your material patent application go to patent pending.'

So Dave went to the Argon National Laboratories and met with Roger Popel, Head of Ceramics and Super-conductivity. When Dave told him his whole story, he said, 'We have physicists here at the national labs that have theorised that the very elements you're are telling us should, do this. We know this already. We just don't have anybody who can make them into that state. We're making them one atom at a time in the nuclear facility and know they exist in this state, but making them one at a time it's going to take years and years to produce enough to evaluate it as a super-conductor.'

So he was very excited about it. He wrote it all up and submitted to the Argon National Laboratories, and their attorneys turned it down. Because, they said, 'It involves chemistry and it can be done without the government lab's involvement. You can go to a private lab to get this done, and our very purpose for existence was to do things that you couldn't get done at a private lab.'

Dave said, 'Roger, the problem is if you don't make the white powder, how do you know it's gold, because you have no machine that will confirm it's gold?' What I have to have is, 'You take gold and change it into white powder so you know it came from gold.' He said 'I see your point Dave, it is a problem isn't it?' He said, 'I'll tell you what, there are two guys who used to work here, I know them personally, I socialise with them, I go places at the weekend with them, I know them real well. I'll write to them, and tell them I want them to make this white powder for you. I know them well enough that, if they say it came from gold, I will accept it as coming from gold.'

So he sent Dave to Mike McNallon and Steve Daniluck over there at High Tech. They told Dave they would do the work for $20,000. They bought the yellow gold, and using his procedure made the white powder. And they acknowledged they didn't know where this stuff came from, because it doesn't analyse to be gold, it doesn't have the properties of gold, but it came out of gold.

So David provided the affidavit to the patent office, all signed sealed and notarised. Now it goes to the Department of Defence and they say, 'That's not enough, now we want to know how you take the white powder and change it back to the yellow metal, gold'. Dave said, 'You must understand this is a materials patent not a procedural patent for the white powder, I was patenting the white powder. I showed them how to make the white powder from a known material, I made an apple into apple sauce, now they wanted me to make the apple sauce into an apple.'

David told them, 'I can do it, but I don't think I want to tell you how to do it.' What it boiled down to was they wanted as much information as possible from him before they gave him the patent. If they got that piece of the puzzle they would know exactly how this phenomenon works. They would get this stuff and put it into lasers and learn how to energise those with DCR and help produce gamma radiation. And that's a weapon you don't want Gadaffi having, or Hussein, or the military. It will go through brick walls and lead; it will kill everybody in the building but not harm the building. It is a very dangerous material, and no one should mess with it.

So in 1993 David Hudson quit pursuing the patent. The attorney said, 'They never can grant a patent to anyone else that will ever apply for yours, because you applied for it and got turned down.' David said that was all he wanted anyway. So after the expenditure of $540,000 he stopped pursuing the patents. So anyone who is searching for his patents and not finding them that's the reason why, all you'll find is 'patent applied for'. David was financially strapped by then, as it was costing a hell of a lot to maintain the patents. He coupled this with the assurance that they could never issue another patent to anyone on his patent, and said, 'Drop it, don't let us pursue it anymore.'

In 1994 his uncle came to him with a book and said, 'This book talks about white powdered gold.' Dave said, 'Oh really I got a white powdered gold and nobody will allow me a patent on it.' His uncle said, 'Dave it's a book on alchemy,' Dave said, 'I'm really not interested in alchemy. I'm a dirt farmer trying to get credibility in physics and chemistry and you bring me a book on alchemy. I'm really not interested in alchemy. Alchemy is when the Church were involved, this is the occult, I'm not interested in that stuff.'

His uncle said, 'But Dave, it talks about a white powder gold, it even talks about gold glass.' Dave said, 'And they are right, it does look like gold glass, it looks clear, it just looks white to the naked eye. But if you heat it in a vacuum at 1,160 degrees it will fuse to a pure glass, it's very brittle, but it will grind back down to the white powder. But it is glass.' Dave was amazed to learn that it talked about this in the alchemy text. It also talked about it being the main container of the essence of life.

'Well, we once said that when we have the analytical method this stuff could be anywhere,' Dave continued. 'Like a stealth atom it could be in anything and no one would know it. So one of the first things we did was to go to Safeways and buy some cow and pigs brains and take them to the laboratories and put them in fuming sulphuric acid and carbonise them, and then oxidise away the carbon and do a metal sulphate analysis on the residue.

'And we found that over 5 per cent of the dry matter weight in the brain was made up of rhodium and iridium in the high-spin state, and nobody knows it. Then we read this text that says it's the container of the essences of life. I thought, gosh is this possible that this is the same white powder that they are talking about? So I began to do medical studies with it. Now I've done physics, chemistry, super-conductivity, quantum mechanics, and now I'm into medicine.

'I went to a doctor and I told him the stories about it, and he began to administer the white powder to a dog. This dog was a golden retriever who had an abscess, valley fever and tick fever. No medicine they had could cure this animal, nothing would work.

'They injected 1 milligram, 1 cc in the tumour on his side, 1 cc intravenously and after a week and a half everything has gone away, and the dog's feeling great. One milligram! That's nothing. That's so small you can barely see it. However, after a week it began to grow back. So they began to inject the dog again, but this time they kept it going for about two weeks and it never came back.'

Then, without telling Dave at the time, the doctor began to give it to an HIV patient.

'The HIV patient was literally so weak he could not eat or speak. He was on his deathbed being fed by IV every two days. The doctor injected 2 milligrams of the powder into his IV. After a week and a half, he is getting dressed on his own, he's eating on his own, and he's thrown away the IV lines, and they have to inject directly into his arm. In a month and a half he's on a plane flying back home to Indiana to attend a family wedding and shaking hands with everybody. They don't even know he's HIV positive.

'You do not get spontaneous remission from HIV. With some cancers you may from time to time, but not with HIV. The doctor was very impressed. So impressed he went on to treat a man who had carposious sarcoma, they are cancers that travel all over your body on the skin. This fellow had 30 lesions over his body. So he injected him with 2 milligram a day and in a month and a half the lesions were totally gone. When the lesions were dry you could literally just rub them away. You may get a slight discoloration where they have been, but the lesions just go. That's with just 2 milligrams a day.'

Dave puts special emphasis on the fact that they were using white powder, made of rhodium and iridium and not gold. Because they discovered that was already in the body, they thought that's what they'd start with. 'Doctors have worked on patients with cancers, ALS, MD, MS, pancreatic cancers, and liver cancers. They have done some experimentation with brain cancers. And one of the things they find is, when the dead tissue of the cancer actually begins to turn to healthy tissue, the cancer appears to get larger, and that's the opening up of the cancer. If you have brain tumours there is a size limitation, you don't necessarily want to use this material so you may want some other way of treating it initially.'

'This remarkable material is now being evaluated by the alternative medicine division of the National Institute of Health in New York City and many other places throughout the United States. And data is being developed on the information discovered. So not only are we talking about a new form of patent, we're talking about a room temperature super-conductor that super-conducts up to 800 degrees.

'The implications for many areas of science are immense. Then to find out that it is a natural constituent of your body and that it literally flows the light of life around your body. People have actually confirmed that there is super-conductivity in your body. The US Navy researchers have measured super-conductivity in your body. What they don't know is what is super-conducting, because it's like some stealth atom that they can't identify. And they're right, that's exactly what it is. It's a higher form of matter that they're not aware of.'

While most scientists today wouldn't know what David Hudson is talking about, some must see its possibilities. Through David's work we now have the ability to take the next step towards free energy. The problem I now see is that scientists themselves will not like the idea that a dirt farmer is able to tell them where they went wrong. And will not want to lose face by having to study work that has gone on outside the scientific fraternity. I hope in the near future to use David's material to heal a friend who has MS. The outcome of this I will make public knowledge so that others can try. I do not intend to let his findings slip away into oblivion.

Through the stress of his work on reaching a conclusion with the white powder, plus government trying to close a factory where he was just starting to try and make the material, David suffered a heart attack and has had a triple by-pass. His doctor and his family are advising him to take things easy, so it is going to be difficult for him to continue with his good work. Many people – myself included – have offered to help, and hopefully when he is better he will accept. Surely we can't get this close to the answer to all our dreams only to walk away.

CHAPTER 13

David Hudson is not the only person to discover a substance or method that can cure many diseases. It seems that the human race has had many chances to heal the world of its ills. So why hasn't it been used? The answer is simple – greed.

If I say the name Dr Royal Raymond Rife M.D, most people wouldn't have heard of him. My doctor being one of them. He was born in 1888 and in the 1930s he invented the most powerful microscope ever to detect diseases His method is still used today. He also invented an instrument to kill diseases to great acclaim. He was even called the saviour of the world by some.

He discovered that all living things resonate and have their own frequency, even diseases. His instrument could be set to the frequency of a disease and with fine tuning it would make the disease break down. It is the same principle as an opera singer who can break a glass with a certain pitch. Nothing else in the room will break unless it has the same frequency. At the time he asked doctors with patients who were terminally ill with cancer to let him experiment on them.

Overseen by the Mayo clinic and a team of scientists and doctors, Dr Rife set up a clinic, sponsored by the University of Southern California, to test his theory of curing cancer, using frequencies alone. Sixteen terminally ill cancer patients – some of them so ill that they had to be brought in by ambulance – came to his clinic. Within 130 days, all 16 walked out of the clinic completely cancer-free and with no side-effects. This great discovery made front-page news. (See picture 25.)

Rife went on to find the frequency of 600 diseases. The medical establishment at that time, along with the pharmaceutical drug czars, saw this discovery as a potential financial disaster for them. The whole medical community turned against him and he died penniless in 1971. Think of all the people who have died needlessly since then – because of money!

Of all the global industries (including oil, gold, banking and the Church) pharmaceuticals is the largest – even governments have to do as they say. After much research Rife machines have now been built again. While doing the research for a proposed TV programme on the subject, we made contact with one of the people working on them.

Believe it or not they are still nervous about the possible

repercussions if and when the drug companies find out it is in use once more. We have also discovered the reason for their nervousness. Laboratories have been burnt down and people have been poisoned. You may ask why we never hear about these things in medical journals. It's purely because the drug companies finance the journals.

I felt the only way to save lives in at least two ways was to get this out into the public domain via TV. The problem then is, is there a TV broadcaster with the guts to broadcast it? If you don't see a programme about this subject on TV in the next 18 months then the answer is no. That being the case there is no hope for the human race on any front that doesn't involve money.

Do people who work in the higher echelons of these drug companies have any scruples? Do they have children? Do they love their family more than money? Do they have family that they have watched die because they know that their drugs cannot heal them?

Or do they know where the Rife machines are (there are only four in the world to our knowledge) and when anybody in their families gets an incurable disease do they send them there to get the only known cure? Maybe because they know there are only four Rife machines in existence they're not a threat to them at the moment. It may be useful to follow drug company czars and their families to find out where they go when they are incurably sick. Do doctors for the royal family know where the Rife machines are? They do seem to live a long time, don't they?

When I read that Tony Blair is going to put billions of

pounds into the National Heath Service and there could have been a cure for everyone using a few pence worth of electricity, it makes me sick to my stomach. When a drug is nearing its sell by date it's the government who foots the bill for the advertising campaigns, not the drug companies. There is really no one in the world now who is looking after our interests. Governments are only looking after their own. If you had a Rife machine at home, by law you or your pets would be the only ones able to use it.

CHAPTER 14

Is there any way we can break this chain of events? I believe there is but it could only happen if the whole world agreed. There was a time before the invention of money when people would barter for everything they needed for survival. If you had more than you needed of something, you may have exchanged it for eggs, butter, milk, bread or whatever you needed.

After a time the system became so complex that the easiest thing to do was to put a value on gold and silver and use it as a currency. It would certainly save people taking cows, pigs and sheep around with them all day in exchange for whatever they needed.

Because money was invented to serve a purpose in those days, does it mean that we always have to use it? I realise you can't uninvent something after it's already been invented, but surely money is nearing the end of its useful life. In fact, it is slowing the progress of mankind at an ever-increasing rate. Mankind has to stop right now and think, Where do we go from here?

We are the only animals on this planet that use money. All other species eat for free. So why should we pay for food? Doctors tell us the human being needs three meals a day to stay healthy. Should anyone – government included – have the right to deny anyone the right to eat? It would be like saying you can't breathe today.

This is how it starts; when you begin to eliminate what we shouldn't have to pay for, you begin to see what is really important in life.

We the human race live on Earth. It is our home collectively and it should not be owned by anyone. Anyone who tells you any different does so for his or her own ends. Kings and queens will say they fought for their land, but they did not, you did (or at least your ancestors did).

If you did the fighting, how is it that they seem to think they own it? Who gave them that right of ownership? They have no more right to it than you do. The native Americans laughed when our ancestors tried to buy land with beads – how can you buy land? they thought. It's like buying the air.

We the human race have been so wrapped up with having to earn money we can't even begin to imagine another way of living. So many new inventions are being created (many of them at the atomic level today) that we could cure the world of all illness within months. This will not happen because it would wipe out the drug companies. Reason – money.

Still at an atomic level we now have the ability to send energy in the form of electricity around the world for free (after the initial and nominal charge of setting it up) This will not happen because of the oil companies. Reason – money.

Without realising it, the governments in England and on the continent are sending our countries back in time, almost to the Stone Age. By joining Europe there is no need to be different from any other nation. We can now live anywhere we like, work anywhere we like, have children with someone of any nationality we like. The melting pot has started again on a larger scale.

It makes one wonder why there were so many wars, when we are on the brink of giving our individuality and/or nationality away! That being the case there was no need to have ever been British! Or any other nationality come to that. Whether we like it or not that has to be the message now. Now when we think in terms of an army – who will they be fighting for? None of us has an allegiance to any individual country because governments have given them away.

Are we now nomads? Well in a way yes we are, exactly like the Native American Indians. We all live on the land and from the land collectively, but we don't own it. From this basis we could begin to develop a society that operates in an entirely new way without the restriction of money. The problem is that to change, the whole world would have to be of the same mind. But where there's a will there's a way.

In 1973, proof emerged that we could live without money and at the time no one could do anything about it. The world could not get enough oil. At the time Edward Heath the

British Prime Minister put the workforce of England on a three-day working week. Everyone complained, large companies moaned because they lost 10 per cent of production. They told the Prime Minister that had he given them more warning they would not have lost anything.

This was a glimpse at a future without money. Because the work force only had to work three days a week and only lost 10 per cent of production, surely this means they worked harder because they only had to work three days a week.

If the average working week at that time was up to six days, then workers were doing a week's work in three days. Hence they were doing one year's work in six months. I'm sure with the help of technology today even that could be reduced to 4 months. At the moment only around a third of the population work, about 18 million people, the rest are too young, too old, too ill, or too lazy.

If the working population were told you only have to work 4 months of the year I believe they would jump at the chance, but only if they made the same money. And rightly so, because they were producing the same quantity. However at this point there is another way.

You tell them by law that they have to work 4 months a year, and they will have 8 months' holiday. They will not get paid, but all that they need to live on will be free. Takes a lot of thinking about doesn't it?

All the questions that arrive out of this statement are phenomenal, but you know I haven't found a question yet that can't be answered. Street level questions are usually the first to emerge.

Question: OK, if I go down the pub, you're saying, I can just go in and say 'Bartender, line up 12 double shots of whisky,' and I can do this every day for free? They'd soon run out of whiskey at our local, I'll tell you that for nothing. And everyone in our village would be pissed for the rest of their lives! No, people would be too greedy, it wouldn't work."

Answer: They can be as greedy as they want. Logically they will not have any more whiskey than anybody else will, who lives for say, 80 years. If someone has a bottle of whiskey every day how long will he or she live? He or she is having their share faster but over a much shorter time. And that goes for anything that is consumed – be it food, drink or drugs.

When in the 1960s, airlines began giving complementary drinks, because of our new-found fame and the fact that we were flying everywhere, some of The Troggs would often get off the aircraft hardly able to string two words together. But that soon passed and we would only have a drink if we fancied one, and not just because it's free and available.

Question: So I can run straight out and get a Rolls Royce?
Answer: Would you need one? Or better still, would we need to build one in the first place? Is it really necessary? If we try to absorb what it

would be like living in a society that has no need for money, then most questions answer themselves. To begin with no money means no one is pushing drugs. You have eradicated the drug problem at a stroke. Most of all petty crimes would cease among teenagers, because it is usually drug related. In fact there would be no need for any crime, except perhaps crimes of passion. Because the crime rate would go through the floor, you wouldn't need a large police force, legal system or prison service. That being the case, look at the amount of people you would release back into the 4-month-a-year work force. Even if you hated your job, 4 months is better than a year.

Question: Would we need government?
Answer: There will always be a need for someone to organise. There is always someone who likes organising! Maybe a new name is needed at this point. The Organisers, or the Guardians. They could still be voted in or out; and because there is no money involved it would stop them from robbing us blind with taxes.

How many people are in jobs they are only doing for the money? This would stop; you would be able to get jobs you liked doing and there would always be someone to fill your place when you were not on your work period, by using a rota system.

Question: How would you get rewarded for work that you did above and beyond the call of duty or if you invented something to benefit mankind, or perhaps you were a talented artist?

Answer: All these things would be rewarded the same as they are today by fame. But the fortune side of it would be to be living in a fortunate society that allows you to eat when you're hungry, drink when you're thirsty, holiday wherever you want, have all that you need, free.

Question: Surely there would be no incentive to work, or at least work well?

Answer: If people were able to do a job they really wanted to do, that would be a real incentive. Don't forget that although by law you would have to work for only 4 months you could please yourself at what. Today, if you're a millionaire there is no need whatsoever to think of money and yet most millionaires work harder than anyone else on the planet because they can do exactly what they want to do. You would all, in effect, become millionaires because you have no money worries. I know one thing for sure, conversations would suddenly become very short – because there would be nothing to grizzle about.

You would have much less waste in manufactured goods that are not really necessary. Hence less pollution. Hence a healthier environment.

> **Question**: Isn't this just Communism?
> **Answer**: Communism and Capitalism are exactly the same thing if taken to their extremes. But both need money for their ideological outcome.

As we have seen, communism was the first to fall, and by the people's unrest every May Day, capitalism will be next, it's just a matter of time. This is because there are too many have-nots in the capitalist system. Middle England will only take so many burglaries, so many muggings, so many rapes, so many murders. The first signs of the disintegration of capitalism will be the lack of people voting, simply because there will be no party worth voting for, because they will just be more of the same, nothing new. We really must have something in place ready to take over! There must never be a void.

The government should be aware and ready for this, but at the moment they haven't a clue how unpopular governments are. They just think people are lazy when it comes to voting. In fact there is talk of them forcing people to vote by changing the law. If this happens I suggest every one of us goes to the polls and votes for the most insignificant political party at the time. It would frighten the major parties to death and would serve them right for not having their ear to the ground and knowing what we really want.

Question: How would we change from the system we now have to the system you're suggesting?

Answer: What I'm suggesting would have to be worked on by a think tank for several years to iron out all the problems that may arise in the beginning. And then, without warning, the change would have to happen overnight. The reason for this would be because of the aggravation you would receive from people with money.

So many things have got to happen before any of all the above could conceivably take place. Firstly the absolute breakdown of law and order, the absolute mistrust of all types of leadership, the abolition of the Church. Isn't it strange that all these things are slowly beginning to happen? So maybe the change may come sooner rather than later.

All the ancient prophecies end on 21 December 2012. I have never believed it to mean the end of the world, but I do believe that it means the beginning of the new.

CHAPTER 15

Until recently we would call old people 'old age pensioners'. Now we say 'senior citizens', a much nicer and uplifting phrase. The mentally handicapped we now call 'people with learning difficulties'. Maybe God can be renamed Mother Nature. If we say 'God will smite you' as they say in the Bible, it's like turning God into a murderer. If we say Mother Nature can kill we know what is meant.

How many battles have been fought in the name of God? If God was one good being, does mankind actually believe he would be with them on all the massacres and rampages that there have been throughout history? It may be more acceptable to say Mother Nature had a hand in it, when the great culls of war have balanced the great numbers of people.

We must never forget that the Church and the Bible were not made by God but by man. Money or possessions have always corrupted mankind, and the Church is no exception. The Church is one of the oldest businesses along with royalty, and it has always been hard to separate the two. Throughout history the Church and the throne have worked closely together. Hence, in most battles you will hear the cry 'For God and country!' Royalty owns our land and the Church owns our spirit. What a winning combination.

When you begin to look back in history to the people the Church has helped, nothing flies out of the pages of the history books at you. The Church has the most land apart from royalty, the most money, the most property and that's the way they want it to stay. To be fair there are exceptions to the rule, people like the late Mother Theresa. One saint among many sinners!

Each time the Church has set sail with their king's armies to new lands, they have helped to destroy every culture they have come in contact with. To make those of us left at home believe that they were taking God's word to all nations they would create stories of confronting heathens that had to be taught a lesson. In most cases, those they encountered were more religious than they themselves were!

Most natives believed in Mother Nature or Mother Earth and were not preoccupied with filling their own pockets. However, the Church had to paint them in the worst light that they could. They could not let the people back home know they were wiping out civilisations with more knowledge than they themselves had. The Church went to great lengths to hide this.

For instance, when the Catholic priests arrived in South

America they discovered that the Aztec and Inca had been playing an instrument that the earlier Mayans had invented. Until then, this instrument was believed by Europeans to be European. It is an instrument (close to my heart, because I played it on 'Wild Thing') called an ocarina. To hide history, they not only made it illegal to play these instruments, but they gathered them all together, dug a huge pit, smashed them up and buried them.

Years later, thousands of ocarinas were found by archaeologists. They, like the priests, told everyone that they were clay candleholders, and that's how it stayed until someone pieced one together and played a tune. How is it a supposedly backward people could make instruments the same as Europeans and yet they had never met? Rather than re-think history, let's bury the evidence, that was how they thought and still do.

The Mayans, Incas and Aztecs knew far more about the stars than the Catholic priests and the Conquistadors that arrived in their country from Europe. So that they could tell the world that they were heathens or devil worshippers, they set about destroying all of the ancient indigenous peoples' works of art, artefacts and books.

Those priests twisted history so that they could continue to line their own pockets with gold. The priests and their actions set history right back, maybe by thousands of years. How dare they use the name of God to do this? However, with modern technology we can rediscover the legacy left to us by the ancient peoples of all continents, despite the Church.

If there are no such things as UFOs, the human race has a

huge problem, because more people believe in them now than in God. Some might say, and rightly so, because there is more evidence of their existence than His. Throughout history, the shock of truth has always weighed heavy on our belief system. The human race thrives on status quo. Once a majority believes something, it takes more than just evidence to change minds.

Until this decade some people still believed the Earth was flat and some people still do, despite all the evidence to the contrary! This belief was perpetuated by the Church, who needed a flat Earth to make heaven and hell work, heaven being up, and hell being down. On a round world there is no up or down. So where is heaven and hell now? Surely if you've done away with hell, you've also done away with heaven.

Had he not been dying at the time, Galileo would have been hung for heresy, for saying the Earth revolved around the Sun, and not the other way round. This was because of the Church's belief that the Earth was the centre of the Universe. The belief in God through the eyes of the Church, has slowed the evolution of mankind's thought to a snail's pace. The Church truly has so much to answer for.

For the first time, people are questioning the Church without the fear of death. So now questioning can be fierce, direct, and without much reprisal. We are finding out that many things we have been taught through the Church simply don't stand up to scrutiny. The first Bible was written 400 years after Jesus' crucifixion. How accurate can that be? Even then we were only given the Church's interpretation of what it said and meant, because they were the only ones who could read.

Surely the time has come to know the truth about our past, and not be asphyxiated by the lies and deceit of a dying cult which thought only of itself. The truth may be shocking, it usually is, but if we face it as one people, how bad can it really be?

If we as the human race need to know the whole story about the beginning of creation and our reason for being, we must have all the evidence. Until then, it's all guesswork. If a court of law does not have all the evidence then there is no case. We are also aware in a court of law what can happen when evidence is unlawfully withheld by the police, or anyone, come to that. For instance the Guildford Four. Three men and one woman imprisoned for 16 years for something that they did not do.

If the courts could get the truth, the whole truth and nothing but the truth, Jeffrey Archer would have gone down 18 years ago. It is difficult enough getting accurate information from history or archaeological digs, so when you have people actually interfering with data, it becomes almost impossible to get at the truth. Some people will deliberately change evidence just for the hell of it, just to see what happens.

I once spoke to a London detective who told me, 'When a murder is committed, we normally get about ten phone calls from people saying they did it. When a bomb goes off somewhere in the country, all the cranks phone in to say they did it.' But when somebody tries to change history, in most cases, it is because of greed.

CHAPTER 16

Many people throughout the ages have tried new ideas, trying to change the nonsensical way we live. Most of their attempts have failed because they have had strange cult connotations. Sometimes they have blatantly gone against religious doctrine, by having demonic undertones. Perhaps it serves the latter right if they were stopped by the powers that be.

However, when someone thinks of a great new idea and wants to try it out and there are none of the above problems involved, surely they should be left alone, and not harassed. Well you would think so ...

Twenty- five years ago a Italian man in his early twenties called Oberto Airaudi (but now known as Falco) persuaded 40 people to dig into a mountain with no more than picks and shovels. He gave them all a dream to build a city in the mountain and a different way of life; they called it Damanhur, which means The City of Light.

After several hundred yards of tunnelling they dug out the first room, which they called The Temple of Mankind and began to make carvings in the rock walls and decorate them. They were not religious but wanted to create a building that celebrated mankind. The land was their own, all they wanted was to be left to do their own thing.

Ten years ago, at 7 o'clock one morning, 400 police and military broke into 40 Damanhur properties simultaneously. With them they brought helicopters and dogs, and the police – mostly anti-terrorist police - were all armed.

The police and military were woken at 3am, put on trucks at 4am, and told nothing about where they were going. However, by the size of the operation it was clear that their bosses were expecting big trouble. Within an hour, they were wandering around trying to work out why they were raiding these harmless people. They realised the raid was groundless and stopped it themselves. The Damanhurians cooked breakfast that morning for 400 police.

An investigation by the Damanhur people at the highest levels revealed that the order for the raid had come directly from the Vatican. Even today, it is still the biggest raid in Italian history – bigger than any Mafia raid.

It goes to show not only what power the Church still has, but also how they regard possible competition. Since that early morning wake-up call many of the police liked it so much they stayed, and are now part of the community.

Much more digging has taken place in the past 25 years and

now they do have their City Of Light. The amazing thing is that floors drop away and produce stairways as they do so, whole walls move to let you pass. My business partner came home raving about it and the friendliness of the people.

They are even experimenting with time travel but can only travel backward in time at the moment. When I inquired as to whether they performed this with their minds, the answer was no, physically. This I have to witness myself. If it is all true it will just go to show what can be achieved when minds work together without the interference of Church and government.

CHAPTER 17

New evidence from America will shed fresh light on abduction. Several operations have now been carried out on abductees, who maintain that in the course of their abductions aboard alien spacecraft, small objects were placed in their bodies. Until now all that investigators have had is the abductees' word for these events, until June 1995 that is. It was then that Derrel Simms met Dr Roger K. Leir.

Dr Leir was shown an X-ray of an implant in a woman's foot. In fact there were two, one in her big toe and the other in her heel. From his experience with foot radiographs, it appeared that the woman's foot had undergone some type of surgical procedure involving the bone. Derrel told Dr Leir that the woman had never had an operation or an accident. The X-ray was taken due to a contiguous problem.

The doctor asked Derrel if he thought the woman would be

prepared to have these objects surgically removed. Derrel said the woman would be overjoyed, but she had no medical insurance. After some consideration, Dr Leir told Derrel that if the woman were flown to California he would perform the operation free of charge. This was all agreed at the 'UFO EXPO WEST' in southern California, where Derrel was speaking.

Derrel told this story to his audience, and asked if anyone could foot the bill for the airfare. Within minutes of ending his lecture somebody had put up the money. In fact a gentleman put up his hand and asked if the doctor would also remove his implant, and later he and the woman were both flown to the doctor's California practice.

Both operations were performed at the same time. Both of these events were captured on video. Since then, Dr Leir has performed many similar operations, and has removed 15 objects at the time of writing. I have been told they are made of meteor dust and a small quantity of gold, but there are other elements that have yet to be analysed.

If all this information is verified and genuine, it may possibly be what forces governments to capitulate. They will have no alternative. We will be able to give the media what they maintain has always been lacking, and that is proof that aliens exist and are here.

No man's quest for the truth about extra-terrestrial beings arriving on this planet can be more dedicated than that of Dr Steven Greer. He has spent a considerable part of his life in search of the answer. Although he has seen and experienced UFOs himself, his ambition has been to let the whole world know.

Throughout the years he tried and has now succeeded in persuading many people to come forward from all walks of life and tell the world what they have seen. It has not been easy. It's taken him ten years, to my knowledge. On 5 May 2001, he called a press conference at the Washington Press Club where 40 people said they would swear on oath before Congress that they had not only witnessed UFOs but, in some cases, been responsible for helping with the cover-up by saying nothing.

These were not your average people in the street. They were high-ranking people from admirals to professors, generals to astronauts, air traffic controllers to lawyers. All ready to swear their involvement to Congress. At last it was released to the world's news media – the 'Disclosure Project' was now under way. No one could stop it now.

It hit Reuters. Reuters then put it out to the world. BBC World News jumped on it immediately. But it was at 3am in the morning that the short, sweet report was broadcast. And even then they sneered by saying something about little green men. What bloody moron read the news that morning at 3am? You may argue that no one with any grey matter between their ears would be reading the news at that time of day anyway, but that's how they reported it – the biggest news item of our time. It's no wonder that minorities suddenly flare up when they keep getting completely ignored.

Dr Greer was going to organise a protest rally if they ignored them, and I hear it was planned for 25 October 2001. But after the events of 11 September it would not have been appropriate. For a while at least, it has lost its impetus.

One of the men to come forward, by means of his book

entitled *The Day After Roswell*, is the late Colonel Phillip J Corso. The story he tells should leave no one in any doubt whatsoever as to the existence of UFOs. Just after the Second World War he was stationed at Fort Riley and witnessed the arrival of alien beings which were placed in a hangar overnight at the base.

After this event he was posted to the Pentagon and it became his job to find a use for artefacts which came off the crashed UFO from Roswell. The way he achieved this was to put them through what they then called foreign technologies. For example if something from Russia or France crashed on or near American soil and they arrived at the site first, then whatever technologies were found, they would have them back engineered to find out their uses.

In the case of UFO technologies it was good for the companies that he chose, because he could offer them patents on the objects. Whatever was discovered from the alien technologies was then sold back to the government. He maintained night sights were gained from these technologies – plus fibre optics, bullet-proof vests, metal with memory, very advanced computer chips, and the technology for the Stealth Bomber.

He remembers playing in the corridors at night with the eye coverings from the aliens and says how well you could see in pitch-black darkness. Colonel Corso's son maintains his father's book was only the tip of the iceberg of what his father knew and had told him.

Many believe the CIA, which was set up at the time of Roswell and some believe because of Roswell, used their new found powers to threaten anyone who tried to open their mouths about the UFO crash at Roswell. Their tactics then – as now, I'm sure – would leave a person in no doubt as to what would happen if they talked.

Civilians were told they would end up buried in the desert. Army personnel, however, were treated in another way, as in the case of a Sergeant Brown whose job it was to take an alien back to the air force base at Roswell. He was told that if he kept the secret until the day he died, Uncle Sam would take care of his family. As he was a good soldier, he kept his word. This piece of information came to light via his two daughters.

For the latter part of his army career, their father was stationed in England and while here he married their mother who was English. After he finished his service he stayed and became an UK resident, and spent the rest of his life here. I met his daughters at the showing of the Roswell alien autopsy footage at the London museum in May 1994, and their story was more than a little convincing.

They told me that when their father was on his deathbed, he told them what happened at Roswell. That an alien craft had crashed and he was sworn to secrecy. He told them because he had kept this secret for Uncle Sam, Uncle Sam was going to take care of them when he died. He gave them a phone number to ring that he had carried with him since the crash. While she was telling me, a tear rolled down her cheek.

She said, 'My father, although dying, had all his faculties. He was not delirious. Would he waste time on his deathbed talking about aliens if it were not true? I knew my father well and he would not.' Later I asked her what happened when she rang the number that her father gave her. She said, 'After the initial shock, the woman on the end of the phone told me to hold and after some time she said they knew nothing about it.'

When pushed harder at a later time they told his two daughters they had no record of their father ever being in the army. This infuriated them because they had all his memorabilia at home and photos of him receiving medals of honour from recognisable army personnel service men. Take note at the way you can be treated by your country. Should you honour your country if this is the way your country honours you? (See picture section).

CHAPTER 18

Some humans cannot conceive of a beginning or end to the universe. As information filters through from scientists to the real world, I find myself unable to take on board their most basic utterances. It is not that I don't understand what they are saying; it's just that it doesn't sit right.

The problem I find with scientists is that they reason beyond all credibility, yet do not pick up on things right in front of their noses. No wonder every ten years or so they have to come up with yet another theory. Scientists seems to have very bad tunnel vision. They only see from one specific angle, missing out on everything else that comes into view. Einstein, brilliant as he was, never twigged that there had to be something faster than light because if there is such a thing as a black hole, as scientists believe, and nothing can escape from it, not even light, then gravity has to be faster to grab the light.

Using scientists' discarded information, I feel I have put together several important pieces of the puzzle of how the universe may begin and end, yet be eternal.

When I was at school, scientists taught us that the Earth probably came from the Sun. This may still be correct if you now know the whole picture. For many years science has embraced the idea of the Big Bang theory, and the black hole. If you put these together you could quite easily have the start of a great idea. Most of science is built around theory. Then you look for answers to those theories.

We must also take into account that most scientists are being paid by the taxpayer, and that if they find answers to questions too quickly they may find themselves out of work. Or looking for something else to ponder over. Have you ever wondered why, when they report a possible new cure for some terrible disease such as cancer or AIDS, they round up by saying it will take another five years for scientists to know if it works. In most cases we are still waiting.

When I first contemplated the black hole, which scientists say exist, it left me with a dilemma. If everything is pouring into it – where is it all going? Yet another question for them to ponder over. Imagine not a hole but a point, a point in space where even light cannot escape.

We have all seen how a car can be crushed down to a cube about 2 feet by 2 feet at the breaker's yard, and dozens of them are thrown onto the back of a lorry and hauled away. Imagine them all being crushed to the size of a pinhead. It doesn't stop there though. Imagine the Earth being crushed to the size of a pinhead. Then the solar system. Then the galaxy. Then all of the galaxies.

Then the universe. All of them crushed to the size of a pinhead. Think of the kind of power or energy required for that to happen.

We all know that energy cannot be destroyed only changed, but into what? Could it be that at this black point in space the change takes place. Is it not also possible, at this point in space, that everything is back in place? All the elements in the universe, all the primordial soup as it were, all at the right pressure for the mixture and ready for the explosion of the Big Bang. Let's face it, if you are missing one ingredient in fireworks they won't go off.

After the Big Bang when everything is released back into space in all directions, away from the point of the Big Bang, it may also be conceived there will be a huge void created, and if my theory has any substance, this void plays a very important role later. You must take into account how many particles (the size of pinheads, which were once planets and galaxies) might react after being crushed to an infinitesimal size.

I believe that just after the Big Bang as they rushed off into space, each speck, each pinhead would try to get back to the size it feels comfortable being. Similar to a bath sponge being held tightly in your hand then released, it returns to the size it once was because the pressure is off. In the case of planets and galaxies expanding rapidly there could also be secondary Big Bangs which may be responsible for the creations of solar systems.

With all the minuscule particles trying to expand to the size of planets, think of the friction that would take place within each fragment. Try to imagine for instance how long it may take a small planet the size of Earth to get from the size of a pinhead to the size it is today. If you think that this is all a bit over the top, there are a few pieces of information slowly coming in from science that could verify what I am saying.

For example, as the *Voyager* probe passed Neptune it sent back information that Neptune was giving out three times more energy than it could possibly be receiving from the Sun. Where was the energy coming from, the scientists asked. They had no idea. I believe the energy is coming from the still expanding planet. Scientists readily agree that the universe is expanding, so why not individual planets?

Whenever we are shown a map of how the world looked when all the continents were joined, we are also shown blue sea all around those continents. We are then shown the continents breaking away from each other and without any more thought we are shown them floating across the deep blue sea, with all the landmasses conveniently gathered on one side of the planet. Easy isn't it? That is if you don't bother to think anymore.

Scientists leave you believing that continents are floating on the sea. We know they are not. So why don't or why haven't they gone into a little more detail and come up with answers to at least one blatant question? How did the continents of America and Africa slide gently 3,000 miles apart? When we know that they are joined beneath the sea. Even if you say, 'Ah, but the continents are floating on magma,' the Earth's crust is hard and is only cracked in certain places which are called plates. Although some plates are diving under others, in the case of Africa and America they are slowly moving apart.

If you look at an ocean floor map of the Atlantic you will see that around 200 miles off the American coast, Africa fits perfectly into contour lines which are visible on the seabed. It's as though a piece of jigsaw puzzle has been taken out, it is so perfect. This taken into account, we should see tell-tale signs on the seabed in the Pacific but there aren't any. If the scientists are right, as we see stretch-marks on the seabed in the Atlantic, we should see wrinkles on the seabed in the Pacific but there are none.

If the Earth were much smaller 200 million years ago, gravity would have had much less pull than today. This could be why dinosaurs were able to grow so big! They did not have so many pounds per square inch on their bodies.

Simon King, a TV presenter, was showing a rock that was reported to be 10 million years old. The rock was broken apart and revealed a seashell inside. He went on to say that it was possible to count the rings on the shell to find out the years, months, and even days of 10 million years ago (like counting the rings of a tree). It was discovered when this creature was alive there were only 347 days in a year. Eighteen fewer than today.

Today we have all noticed that now we are on atomic time we get an extra long beep when the radio gives us a time check. They say this is because the world is slowing down. However, this could be because the Earth is getting larger, and hence revolving faster. We may still take the same time to make the journey round the Sun. But if the world is rotating faster on its axis, then there will be more days in a year or, put another way, more revolutions in the same amount of time. So our years might not be getting any longer it may just be because there are more days in the same period of time. If the world is getting larger this could also account for the reason scientists say the

Moon is moving further away from us! It has to renew or update its position in relationship with Earth's new gravity all the time.

I believe that the Earth is still expanding and one day we will lose that long beep on the atomic clock and gain an extra second. The bigger the Earth becomes the faster it will spin. This means in 20 million years' time there will be 401 days in a year. The Earth, on the edge of its galaxy, is still on its outward journey from the Big Bang, but not for much longer.

Evidence is now mounting from astronomers that there are galaxies on a journey towards us. The Hubble telescope is starting to confirm this. But not to worry, if my theory is correct there were many Big Bangs in space. Not all of them happened at the same time and not all at the same distance from us. But all of them caused outward expansion.

I believe one day there will be a coming together of these remnants of distant Big Bangs and their debris or galaxies, but they will not collide. As our planets in our solar system have found their place in space and do not collide, so too will all the other galaxies have their space! As galaxies come closer to us and we to them, I believe the universes will push at one another. When this power becomes too great, at a certain point of equilibrium, the void which each universe left behind at the time of its creation, will begin to drag back all that left it.

Then, when all is back in place, yet another Big Bang will take place. And so on, *ad infinitum*. Like our lungs breathing in and out to give us life, so the Big Bangs create life on those tiny fragments that leave it. We survive on part of the journey out and part of the journey back. There is no beginning and there is no end.

CHAPTER 19

So to sum up with the evidence that is now in the public domain:

In the beginning there was a Big Bang. Planets the size of pinheads shoot out in all directions, individually expanding as they leave. Solar systems form in their galaxies. They begin to cool, but not all at the same time. Life begins on appropriate planets. Earth is among the last to cool and accept life. Many other planets harbour life long before Earth.

Civilisations on other worlds are up and running. And travelling around in search of neighbours, they find them dotted around the galaxy. Some are equally as advanced as themselves. They join forces to tour the galaxy, and find life and other planets suitable for life. Between them, they believe it is wrong to push life forms too far ahead, even though they could do so. So they watch their development and nurture them gently.

They also experiment on planets that could harbour life. They set up different stages of development in human forms, and believe the information gathered will help their existence. They find our solar system; they start life on Mars. When the Martians reach a certain level of technology a large asteroid hits them, and life begins to fail.

A few wealthy Martians are able to leave Mars in spacecraft. They are allowed to do so by the overseers (the alien federation, who they know nothing about) and come to Earth in a few spacecraft. When they arrive they land in every corner of our planet. They bury the craft they came in and build giant megaliths over them at special places of significance, in relation to where they came from and to the stars that point the way to their old home.

The sites they choose are important to their knowledge of the stars and have to be remembered for later use, when they are again able to build a civilisation capable of returning to them. Their ability to build giant buildings is immediately put to use in places such as Egypt (at the Giza plateau), South America (where the Mayan Temples are situated), Stonehenge and Avebury.

They design the structures using the geometrical technology they will need at a much later date. So it must be built to last, and so to be remembered. Earth, unbeknown to them, is a very unsuitable planet and is upset every so often because it is in the path of heavy meteor showers and asteroids.

In fact the upheavals are so great they almost wipe them out. There are then so few of them that it is forgotten who built the megaliths and where they came from. The monuments themselves remain to be wondered about by the few who survive.

They believe the gods left them as burial sites for their kings, so the true purpose of the megaliths is lost on them. When civilisation finally crawls back to the level it was once at, and we rediscover their true meaning, these megaliths will once again become important to that civilisation.

The answers to inter-planetary travel are wrapped up in these monuments and have yet to be decoded. The time is coming soon when all that we need to know will be rediscovered. Let us hope it's before meteors and asteroids hit us and we have to move on. And where would we move to? Will the alien overseers let it happen? Or have they already started to save us knowing that we are not yet ready to travel the large distances necessary for our survival?

Could it be that when people see alien spacecraft sucking water out of lakes, reservoirs, springs and paddy fields it will be put back by them when the waters of our planet have been polluted to the point of being irreparable by our technology?

Since mankind began to look into rock strata for clues to life on this planet, it has become apparent that nowhere in those strata are there any signs of the ancestors of cattle, pigs or sheep. Could it be that the overseers realised our needs and placed cattle here solely for our purposes? Docile meat machines. Could this be the reason for what are now called 'cattle mutilations'?

Many farmers, especially in America, have discovered cattle on their land which have had their organs removed with surgical precision. Investigation suggests that some kind of surgical tool which we don't possess may have been used. Even the nerve ends are missing and there is no blood left near or in the body. Is some kind of test in progress? After all, if you were planning to restock the Earth at a later date, wouldn't it be wise to check what has been happening to these grass-eaters since we started dropping nuclear bombs 50 years ago? If the overseers can alter genetics and put things right then perhaps that is what is happening. The whole picture is yet to unfold; I hope we are all here to see it.

It is in the human race to explore, especially with our minds. There is no harm in this. Everyone should have that right, no matter how off-the-wall their ideas. Some of the craziest things have become fact. There is a very fine line between fact and fiction. If it is in man's mind it is possible. For every crop circle that appears there are some people that will come forward to say that they did it, but when confronted by the press they deny it. If they owned up, farmers would sue them.

The Wessex sceptics will keep on insinuating that they did the more complex variety, but again they are cautious in case they get sued. All that aggravation for a few minutes of fame in front of the cameras. When Doug and Dave were making one of their simple circles, a large lump of blue ice fell from the sky and cut Dave's head open. Now we all know the ice, more than likely, came from the toilet of an airliner. Is that a coincidence, or was it a higher intelligence saying, 'Don't screw with us'? It could be said it was definitely guided to the right head.

If an alien civilisation has been slowly trying to contact us (slowly, so as not to scare the living daylights out of people), they're not having much luck so far. The majority of humans are too thick to realise that messages are being left in our fields. Most are too preoccupied with making a buck. If an alien craft landed outside the Houses of Parliament tomorrow, I am sure the government would try to say, 'it was one of ours'.

The press would believe them and write what they were told to. If an alien was brave enough to get out of his craft he would probably get mugged. In certain cases I have heard about alien craft being fired at by airforces around the world. If you were an alien would you land here? I love animals, especially gorillas, but I wouldn't get in a cage with one.

Western man has had everything his own way for a very long time. He has devastated other civilisations and cultures, mostly out of greed. He has always thought of himself at the top of the evolutionary tree, and the more power he has the further up the tree he thinks he is. But you'll see many changes if aliens are coming here. Man will no longer know how far up the evolutionary tree he is. I believe he cannot handle that thought – especially if he's a politician.

So that is one of the main reasons for dismissing aliens out of hand. Has he got a surprise coming to him! For the first time in his existence he will be the underdog. He will have to listen and be told. The old cultures of our planet already know how to respect Mother Nature. The Western world has yet to learn. For those who think that they are higher up the evolutionary tree than anyone else is, the change will be harder. Some may not be able to cope with that. The change must come, though. The sooner the better for the sake of our planet.

We cannot carry on in the barbaric ways we have been. It has to end before Mother Nature plays her hand, to save herself from the destruction that we have created. Mother Earth will always be here, humans are transient. She can always find a way that does not include us. If you don't believe this, just ask a dinosaur.

This is not
THE END.
This is
THE BEGINNING.

FURTHER
INFORMATION

For further reading and up-to-the-minute information, try the following:

Bloodline Of The Holy Grail – by Laurence Gardner
Published by HarperCollins
ISBN 0007142943

Genesis Of The Grail Kings – by Laurence Gardner
Published by Fairwinds USA
ISBN 10987654321

Realm Of The Ring Lords – by Laurence Gardner
Published by HarperCollins
ISBN 0007142935

Destiny Of The House Of Gold– by Laurence Gardner
Published by HarperCollins
ISBN 007142951

The Day After Roswell – Col. Phillip J. Corso
Published by Pocket Books
ISBN 067101756X

The Aliens And The Scalpel
Published by Granite Publishing
ISBN 1893183017

Nexus magazine
Published in Australia and the UK

Nexus Magazine
PO Box 30
Mapleton
Queensland
4560
Australia

Nexus Magazine
55 Queens Road
East Grinstead
West Sussex
RH19 1BG
Telephone: 01342 322 854

Websites:
www.disclosure.org
www.cropcircleinfo.com
www.cropcirclefootage.com
www.busty-taylor.com/cropper/98busty2.htm
www.davidpenfound.com